The Teen Popularity Handbook

The Popular Teen Presents:

The Teen Popularity Handbook

Make Friends, Get Dates, And Become Bully-Proof

Jonathan Bennett and David Bennett

Cover design: Meg Syverud (megsyv.com)

Images on pp. 218-220: Joshua Wagner (conflictmechanic.com)

All other images: David Bennett

The Popular Teen logo: Natalie Howard (nhoward.com)

Body language model: Natalie Howard

Theta Hill Press

Lancaster, Ohio

thetahillpress.com

Theta Hill Press

ACKNOWLEDGMENTS

SHOUT OUTS AND THANKS

Jonathan

I'd like to give a special shout out to my family: Carmela, Brianna, and Grace. I'm grateful for their patience as I put the time and energy into writing this book. I'd also like thank my grandparents and parents, who taught me how to be popular while still having values.

Joshua Wagner deserves a special mention since he taught me a lot about humor, routines, and many other things. He was a great "model" from whom I learned a ton.

I also want to express my thanks to Dave Adams who always reminds me to stay on the right path and taught me many other valuable tips as well.

I want to offer thanks to the many parents, students, and

colleagues who supported me during my teaching days. I'll be forever grateful for the love and kindness I received from all of you.

Two people deserve a special mention for agreeing to look over the book during its final revision: Justyn Greene and Andrew Chwalik. I'm grateful for their feedback.

David

I want to thank my wife Jennifer and daughter Elizabeth. My parents and grandparents deserve a shout-out as well, because their genetics and upbringing made me the stable, fun, handsome, popular (and modest) guy I am today.

Joshua Wagner has been a great asset in formulating ideas for this book and for succeeding at life. The many hours Jonathan, he and I spent coming up with models of success made this book possible.

I'd also like to thank David Adams, whose re-discovery of the joys of living coincided with my own.

Also, many thanks to Justyn and Andrew for the reasons Jonathan mentioned. And special thanks to Rachel West and Maureen McCann for their insights and feedback. Also, there are many other students, colleagues, teachers, and friends who have made me what I am today. I have tried to model the best traits from a lot of people.

CONTENTS

Yes, You Can Be Popular

Can you imagine walking down the hallways of your school with your head held high, as your classmates smile at you, hand you notes, and invite you to the best parties?

Can you imagine being the center of attention everywhere you go? Your friends can't believe that there always seems to be a line of strangers wanting to meet you.

Can you imagine having a great social life? Every night you want to go out, three or four friends are practically begging to be at your side. And, that special girl (or boy) just can't wait to meet up with you.

Can you imagine getting invited to every party, having unlimited opportunities at school, home, and work – and getting tons of new contacts on social media all the time – because people like you and find you exciting?

Can you imagine being popular, not because you are some phony, but because everyone loves you just for being you?

Since you're imagining the possibilities, think how great it would feel to give a class presentation with absolute confidence. Also, how exciting would it be to go into a college or job interview with the communication skills to "wow" any recruiter or potential employer?

If you can't really imagine these scenarios, don't worry. You're not alone for thinking you'll never be popular. Maybe you're lousy at sports, you have too many zits, or you've been painfully shy since you peed your pants at recess in the third grade.

Guess what? None of that matters. You don't need to be the star of a sports team or have clear skin to be liked. And, even famous people have had embarrassing moments. You can be popular no matter what you look like and whatever your past. Even if right now you're in your bedroom sulking about your boring life, that doesn't mean you can't be the most popular person at school (and elsewhere) in a few months.

I know because I've walked this path. When I was younger, I was popular and loved by teachers and classmates alike. Even in elementary, I was the leader of men (well, at least boys) at recess and did stand-up comedy every Friday in second grade (I called it "Jonathan's Prime Time Funnies"). Too bad YouTube wasn't around then. Although I had my ups and downs like we all do, I continued being very popular throughout high school. But, after I graduated from college, I fell into the rut of being a "normal" adult. In other words, I had turned into a boring guy that no one paid attention to. My edge was gone. I no longer had the thrill and joy of popularity.

In my early thirties, I had some life events knock me down. I became depressed and angry. I wasn't sure about my purpose or place in this world. However, after a few weeks of pouting, I finally woke up and realized that my life needed a radical change. I didn't want to be "average" any longer. I wanted to be a confident, happy, and exciting person, the guy I was in my youth.

Through my research and practice of successful techniques, and my friendship with David Bennett, Joshua Wagner, and David Adams, I left old patterns behind and became a totally new person. I now live an exciting and fulfilled life and a big part of it is because I am popular and loved everywhere I go.

You may be thinking: "What does this guy know about teenagers? He's old!" First, I'm not old (it's relative). Second, being a teenager hasn't changed all that much since I went to high school. Third, before I went into the popularity business and started writing this book, I was a teacher, and not just any teacher, but a popular one who had the respect and even friendship of my teenage students. You may not know any, but I was a popular and loved teacher.

I observed teens in action every day, watching how they talked to each other and played the social game. I even played that game with them, using my humor and "people skills" to reach them on both social and academic levels. I saw how they succeeded and failed at the task of winning over people. I saw what worked and what didn't. I even helped them get over their hang-ups and become more popular.

The techniques in this book aren't just based on theory, however. I apply them in an adult environment every day, and I am a popular guy who is the center of attention wherever I go. I'm not in the movies, a musician, or a sports star, but I still receive the many benefits of being popular: tons of friendships with both men and women of all ages, an amazing social life, and even lots of free stuff. Yes, total strangers offer me free stuff every day just for being me. You can have all this too.

Since your experience of so-called popular people may not be the most positive, I should say a few words about the kind of popularity this book teaches. I will help you make friends, get dates, and attract people of all types into your social circle. You will learn to make yourself more excellent, and in the process, cut through the drama, stand up to bullies, and enrich the lives of others. I explain how you can be wildly popular while still being positive and inclusive – and live according to your chosen values. If you want to become a bully, this book isn't for you. However, I will teach you how to deal with the bullies and even make them your friends.

I also want you to genuinely change yourself – for the better. It is my hope that you will develop a better self-image from reading this book, because you will be totally transforming yourself. In other words, I want you to become the person you always knew you could be. And when you become that person, it will feel great.

Since David (my twin brother and co-author) and I are men, the book is written primarily from a male perspective. If you are a female reader, don't let that scare you off. Drawing on my years of teaching experience with teens of both sexes, I try to address female needs and challenges as best as possible. However, keep in mind that the male and female paths to popularity (both for friendships and dating) will be slightly different. I will get more specific later in the book.

I encourage you to read this book slowly. Don't rush just to say you've finished it. It's not your summer reading book. Really focus on each chapter. However, for convenience, I reference past and upcoming themes throughout the book. This is so you can either go back and review for more clarity or jump ahead if needed. Also, it's extremely important that you practice the techniques I give you and actually do your assignments.

Yes, I give a form of "homework." But, it's only because the techniques needed to become popular take practice. While the process of bettering yourself may be difficult at times, the information here will, if you master it and incorporate it into your life, change you completely. You will be popular. That's worth the price of a little homework, right?

We have a special offer for you. If you sign up for our mailing list, you can download a free companion workbook. It will help you with your "homework" and give you a record of your progress. In short, it will make you even more popular more quickly. Go to thepopularteen.com/workbook for more information and to sign up.

CHAPTER 1

NO ONE IS BORN POPULAR

When I was younger, I knew a guy who was 6' 7" tall. All of his basketball coaches would practically salivate over him at the start of every season. But, each year his tall butt sat on the bench. Yet, Anthony "Spud" Webb, who stood at around 5' 6" tall, was a successful player in the NBA. Yes, that's right; a guy that short played professional basketball.

The tall guy I knew was a "natural born" basketball player, but he sucked. Webb, who was nobody's idea of a natural, through practice and hard work, made himself into a basketball star. He had his name on t-shirts, lots of ladies on his arm, and tons of dollars in the bank. Oh, and did I mention this "short" dude won the slam dunk contest in 1986? Check it out on YouTube.

Webb's life tells us an important truth about not only sports stars, but every person: you become who you are, not through your situation at birth, but through your effort (or lack of it) and your choices.

I'm not going to get into a debate about genetics. Save that for science (or sociology) class. However, your genes can obviously help or hinder your goals. Spud Webb probably had to work a lot harder than LeBron James, who was gifted with a freaky combination of height and athleticism. But, the fact that Webb made it to the NBA at all proves that anyone, with enough passion and effort, can achieve his or her dreams and become successful even at something that may seem impossible.

Someone who may not have the most advantages in life may even be better off in the long run. My acquaintance from high school was so tall that coaches were always praising him and telling him of his awesomeness. So, what did he do? He dogged it at every practice and behaved like he didn't have to earn a spot on the team. And many times, he didn't. At least not a starting spot. I'm sure Spud Webb encountered a lot of doubters throughout his entire basketball career, from high school right up to the pros. As a result, he was motivated to work harder than everyone else.

When it comes to teenage popularity, it can seem like how you're born makes all the difference. Some people may be naturally more outgoing, better looking, taller, more athletic, and so on. But, it doesn't matter because ultimately being popular requires action. That's right, action. A "naturally" handsome guy who sits at home playing online games all day will never be popular. Same goes for a "naturally" beautiful girl who never hangs out with other human beings. But, a shy, average looking person who vows to be popular and follows this commitment with learning, practice, and never giving up, will, in the end, be far more likely to achieve popularity.

For many people, the "genetics" excuse is just that, an excuse. And it seems like a great one, since our genetics can't be changed. The short boy can exclaim for all to hear that he's not tall enough to get a girlfriend, even though short guys get cute girls all the time. The shy, average-looking girl can claim guys never approach her at parties, although similar girls get more attention than they know what to do with.

No one is born popular. Say that out loud right now (if you're alone). The most popular guy in school didn't come out of his mom's belly good-looking, smart, and funny. Likely, he works hard to stay in shape, studies to keep up his grades, and practices his humor all the time. How often do you make an effort to be popular? Oh, and whining to your friends about being unpopular doesn't count.

By reading this book, you've made an important first step. You're recognizing, even if subconsciously right now, that luck and fate don't determine your level of popularity. You have realized that the power to be a popular teenager is found only within yourself. Hmmmm, you probably didn't think your purchase of this book told me that much, did you?

Now that you're feeling good about yourself, I'll burst your bubble a little bit. Reading a book about becoming popular won't make you popular any more than reading a book about vampires will get you a date with Kristen Stewart. As I mentioned in the introduction, it's going to require practice. Don't worry; this kind of practice will be fun and very rewarding. It will also require work. If being popular were easy then every teen at your school would be popular (which would mean that no one would really be popular).

By following the suggestions in this book, you are working towards an exciting goal: popularity. The best things in life always take some effort and this is no different. Remember, you've likely been unpopular or less than popular most of your life. It may take a while to undo your past patterns and behaviors. So, decide now if you really, really want popularity. If the answer is "yes," then the techniques in this book will help you.

Your practice assignment for this chapter seems pretty easy. You have to believe that even you can be popular. Get over your old hang-ups and issues and start to believe in yourself. That's right, starting today you, yes, even *you*, are on the path to popularity. Think about that for a while.

CHAPTER 2

YOU CONTROL YOUR DESTINY

I used to work with a lady who complained about everything, from the coffee in the break room to the attitudes of the students she taught. At the start of the school year, she moaned about the heat, while in the winter she complained about how she wished it were summer. Once, when a student bought her a plant for her birthday, she told me that the vibrant, deep-red flowers looked too purple, and purple made her sad. Can you believe some people?

Every day, we make many small choices that can lead to some pretty large consequences. These small choices add up to a big thing called "perspective." This is the way we view the world – our mentality, so to speak. Using perspective, our brains make sense of everything around us. My former co-worker had a negative perspective, so everything she encountered was a chance to complain.

On the other hand, the brain of a curious, happy, and fun-loving person would see the same things my co-worker saw and likely love them.

You control your path.

The good news is that a mentality or perspective doesn't have to be set in stone. Through effort, anyone can change how he or she views the world. After all, I don't know a person yet who was born an angry, uptight, and depressed teenager (or adult). By the way, I am getting to the part about being popular, so bear with me. This is important stuff.

The first step to change your perspective on life is to decide what mentality you want. Yes, it's that simple (although putting it into practice can be more difficult). Then, you make your everyday choices based on your desired mentality. The second step is extremely important. Simply saying, "I want to be chill and laid-back all the time," but freaking out every time life throws you a curveball is pretty much pointless.

Most of our lives are lived without even thinking, so to change a mentality we must turn off "auto-pilot" and steer a new course. Let's use the example of taking a chill mentality. If someone you dislike posts something dumb about you on Instagram, your automatic response may be to get angry and start a back-and-forth online brawl, especially if you've reacted that way a thousand times before.

But, to be successful at your new goal, you'll have to turn off auto-pilot and take charge of your brain. Now, you'll take a deep breath and delete this follower, avoiding all of the drama and stress. And, you'll resist the urge to text her or gossip about her to your friends.

What all this means is that you create your own destiny. If you think life is wonderful and the world is beautiful, then guess what? It will be. On the other hand, if you think life sucks and the world is ugly, then even the most beautiful thing like an amazing red flower will seem flawed. Why? Because everything is mentality and perspective. Everything. Your brain, not your eyes, determines how you see the world.

If you are reading this book, you're probably not in what I call the "popular mentality" yet. Maybe you're shy, awkward, dramatic, or hopelessly uptight. Whatever your traits, this book can help you. I was naturally extroverted as a child and teenager, but I developed all sorts of hang-ups as I got older, that stopped me from being fun and popular as an adult. However, applying the techniques in this book transformed me into a guy people want to be around and who gets the perks and benefits of popularity everywhere. And, all I have to do is show up and have a good time doing what I love.

The best way to get into the "popularity mentality" is to follow the advice in this book and practice our techniques every single day. Think again about those little decisions you make on a regular basis. Well, from now on you will be making yours from the perspective of a popular person. Everywhere you go, and with every choice you make, ask yourself how a popular and attractive person would act, and then do that.

I know it's easier said (or read about) than done. If you're not popular, you may not know how to act like a popular kid. Don't worry; this book will explain that. I want you, however, to use your brain to your advantage and start thinking like you're already popular.

I'd like you to write a series of goals. I know you may have done this in school and hated it. But, this isn't to get your guidance counselor off your back. It's to make you popular, so get writing. Write these goals or affirmations in the present tense, but use the language of process. Pick something like "I am becoming popular and making the football team." It's better to affirm that you are becoming, manifesting, materializing, etc. your goals because if you say, "I am popular and on the football team," your brain will counter with "yeah right." However, as you become more popular, you can change your goals at any time.

You should also follow your goals with "declarations." These are statements that declare what you are going to do. Rather than saying what you are hoping to become, these are statements of intent, promises to yourself that you are going to achieve the goals you outline. Use the language of commitment here. Say something like, "I commit to be popular," or "I commit to make the football team." Obviously, your declarations and goals should complement each other.

You can then repeat your goals and declarations out loud throughout the day. One little trick I've found is to record a few short affirmations and declarations, and play them back when you get quiet time, maybe before bed. If recording, use the "you" form in this case. Say, "You are becoming more popular each day." You can then recite them out loud using the "I" form. However, don't say them aloud around other people or they may think you're weird. And, this brings up a valuable point. What you're doing in this book can be a secret. It's no one's business that you're reading it or trying to better yourself.

By stating your goals and making a commitment to popularity each day, your perspective and the choices you make will begin to change as well. For example, I love staying in shape, but sometimes find it hard to exercise. Now, every morning I say, "I commit to exercise and get excited about exercise." When I get tired or lazy, I remember my commitment and am more likely to get my butt to the gym or out on a trail running. The more you say your affirmations and declarations, the more likely this will occur for you too. You're essentially reshaping your values.

Right now, you may not actually believe what you're saying. It may be difficult for you to think of yourself as a popular person admired within your school. This doubt is perfectly normal. However, by regularly affirming and declaring your goals, you are convincing yourself of their truth. Think of the cheerleaders at the football game. They get everyone pumped up and excited, even if the team is lousy. These goals and commitments do the same for your brain. They fight your negative thoughts to help you grow into the person you want to become.

Your assignment for this chapter is to write around five to ten goals/affirmations and declarations and say them every day. If you feel up to recording them, I would advise that too. Convert them to an mp3 format and listen to them on a portable player. I've included some samples below. As you read this book, you will want to modify your goals to include what you learn in future chapters.

Sample Affirmations

I am attracting a new friend each day.

Every day I am becoming more outgoing, exciting, and funny.

I am becoming relaxed, cool, and chill.

I am receiving the benefits of popularity every day.

Declarations

I commit to being outgoing and funny each day.

I commit to waking up in a great mood.

I commit to making at least one new friend every day.

I commit to go out with friends every Friday and Saturday night.

If you want to know more about the role affirmations and declarations can play in your life, as well as how to write them to achieve the best results, check out Say It Like You Mean It: How To Use Affirmations and Declarations to Create the Life You Want written by David and me, with contributions from our good friend Joshua Wagner.

CHAPTER 3

DON'T LIKE YOUR BRAIN? GET A NEW ONE

I recently visited a mall in Columbus, Ohio to do some shopping and meet some friends. Several years ago I had visited that same mall and was at a miserable point in my life. I moped around, wouldn't make eye contact with anyone, couldn't stop thinking about the dreams that had slipped away, and even refused to shop because I was too fat to fit into clothes that I liked.

However, this most recent visit was completely different. I was smiling and confidently approaching people to interact with them. Girls were eyeing me and giggling as I walked by, and I was talking to and laughing with several strangers. While I waited for my friends, I sat down with a cup of coffee at Starbucks and just thought for a few minutes about how amazing my personal transformation had been. I was a completely different person. My body language had changed radically and my mentality had completely shifted. I literally saw the world in a different way.

In spite of the last chapter's talk of goals and transformation, you may be a lot closer to the guy in the first paragraph. Maybe you feel like you can never catch a break with the popular crowd, or perhaps you've gone fifteen years of being unpopular and can't see the light at the end of the tunnel. Even if you're in a pretty deep rut, don't be discouraged. Change is possible! The Jonathan Bennett of the first paragraph didn't become the Jonathan Bennett of the second paragraph magically. Nope, he did it through the techniques in this book and it took a while.

You're going to get a biology lesson now, but I'll try to make it as easy as possible. Scientists have long known that the brains of children are "neuroplastic," meaning that their brains can re-wire as circumstances change. This explains why your little brother can become fluent in a language quickly while you have three years of high school Spanish and can barely say, "Hola."

As a teenager, your brain isn't as changeable as a young child's. Incredibly, a child can lose half of her brain and still pretty much develop normally (1). Let's just say that if you and I lost half a brain we'd be in trouble. However, as a teenager, your brain is still growing and developing. In fact, other than when you were really little, your brain is changing now more than ever.

Let me give you an example of how impressionable the teen brain is. I was a fat pre-teen: I ate too much and exercised very little. I absolutely hated my life as "the fat kid." However, when I was fourteen, I started reading about health. Any book or magazine article I found on health and fitness, I read and tried to put into practice. I lost the weight and became fit. Even now, at my "old age" of thirty-five I have little trouble getting fit and keeping weight off. If I gain it back (which I have before, as paragraph one indicates), I just lose it with little effort.

My friends are shocked. They think losing weight is sooooo tough. And, for them, it probably is. But, I learned how to get fit and healthy when my brain was at its second most adaptable phase and it shows to this day. Your job is to take advantage of your young and adaptable teen brain and learn patterns of confidence and popularity, replacing the old patterns that are unhelpful (like my "fat" patterns). You are not only learning to become popular now, but you're also setting up a solid foundation of success and popularity for the rest of your life.

Even though your brain can be easily changed, it still has a lot of hard-wired patterns and habits, many of them stemming from childhood. Some of them are probably unhelpful. Perhaps your father abandoned you when you were little, so now you distrust men. Maybe you constantly heard from your first grade teacher that you were in the "dumb" reading group, so you never aimed high and are still struggling in school. I'm sure you can think of many more. These beliefs are now literally (and physically) embedded in your mind through brain wiring.

If unhelpful patterns and habits wired your brain in the first place, it follows that the best way to re-wire the brain to be popular is to create new habits to replace the old ones. This is why it's vital to affirm your goals frequently and to act like a popular person at all times, even if you don't truly believe it right now. This repetition constantly tells your brain that you *are* popular, like the cheerleaders getting a bored crowd into the game. Over time, you will actually feel and act like a popular person naturally because you will have convinced your brain that you are popular. This is often called "fake it 'til you make it."

Break down the fences your brain creates and life will improve.

The best way to fight this old wiring is to use a method called re-framing. A frame is another word for mentality. Re-framing, then, is getting a new mentality (see Chapter 2 for review). For example, most people complain when they get rained on. However, whenever David notices someone complaining about the rain, he humorously points out that people actually pay good money to get wet at water parks. Why don't we enjoy the chance nature gives us to get wet for free?

Can you see how this is a re-frame? It is changing one's mentality about a situation (in this case, getting wet) from a negative outlook to a more positive one.

If you find your old ways of thinking re-emerging, then you will need to mentally re-frame the situation. Let's say you see a girl (or guy) you really like. Your old patterns may say to put your head down and avoid the person. However, that's not the new and popular you.

The new you will re-frame the situation by holding your head high, making eye contact, and smiling at your crush. You do this because you have a new, popular mentality. And, over time, your brain will literally change so much that the wiring and firing patterns will be completely different. You will, in many ways, have a completely "new" brain, one that helps you in your quest to meet friends and become popular.

For this chapter, your assignment is to continue saying your goals and declarations and applying what you've learned so far. This means trying out some of the material in this book at school, work, or even home. You may not like them, but parents, brothers, and sisters are at the very least good practice (not target practice either). Changing your thoughts and your actions is the best way to re-wire the brain and become the popular person you know is trapped deep inside of you.

CHAPTER 4

JUST DO IT (YOUR BEST)

A good friend of mine in high school had some trouble meeting women. He was friendly enough and generally liked, but not truly popular. A few of us helped him find a date for Homecoming his junior year. However, he was pretty shy. His date obviously wanted to dance, but he didn't have the courage to ask her out on the dance floor. He kept saying he'd wait until "the time was right."

Finally, on the last song, a mutual friend literally dragged him out on the floor to dance with his date. He loved the experience and expressed regret that he hadn't taken the initiative at the beginning of the evening. My friend isn't alone in his thinking; just take a look at the statements below:

"I'll join the volleyball team next year, when I'm in better shape."

"I'll ask that pretty girl on a date next week."

"I'll be more reliable with my next job."

What do these statements have in common? They all put off for tomorrow what should be done today. These were excuses that I actually heard as a teacher. And, let me tell you a few facts about the endings to these stories. The girl never joined the volleyball team and the guy never went on a date because the young woman had already been asked by another, more confident guy. Oh, and the slacker had no money that summer because no one from his old job would write him a reference. None of these people (or my friend from high school) realized an essential truth until it was too late: change begins right now.

I had the opportunity to hear actor Brian Stepanek of Disney's *The Suite Life of Zack and Cody* speak a few years ago. He told a great story about how, as a struggling actor, he had the chance to headline his own show in Chicago. He felt that after years of hard work performing in smaller venues he had at last arrived as an actor. The first night he didn't exactly play to a packed house. In fact, he played for one freaking person.

He was naturally disappointed and could've easily given up and said, "I'll try again...in the future." But he didn't. He performed the entire show for that one person with the same passion he would've given a full theater. Stepanek said that he stayed on the stage because he loved what he was doing and he was never going to give up his dreams. Brian Stepanek did the best he could (and the guy in the audience even stayed for the second half). He knew, like all of the most popular and successful people, that he couldn't wait until the perfect time arrived, because "the perfect time" never comes.

In addition, all successful and popular people know if they can't be something now (like generous, happy, or funny), then they will never become it in the future. Jesus, the founder of the Christian religion, told a story about a master giving his slaves various amounts of money to invest. Those who had little cash, but used it wisely, received more money at the end of the day. However, those who couldn't even wisely use a measly dollar got nothing. It's a great lesson for life.

The same is true for you. If you can't be fun, happy, cool, witty, and popular at your current school and with your current friends (and your family), then you never will at college, in Hollywood, or in the future. Do any of your friends (or maybe you) fantasize about playing guitar in a giant stadium, but can't even get up the nerve to play at the high school talent show? Here's a hint: if an aspiring guitar hero can't play in front of fifty, he won't be able to play for fifty-thousand.

Your goal is to be the best you can be starting now. Even if you have a small group of friends at school, and work a boring job flipping burgers on the weekends, you still can practice being popular. Make your friends think you're awesome. Throw your charm on the annoying customers and your bored co-workers. When you can become cool and popular in front of your three friends, ten co-workers, and sixty customers, then you're ready to conquer your school.

Your homework for this chapter is to simply start doing your best right now. Examine your list of goals and declarations and think of ways you will start living your list right now. For example, if you wrote, "I am becoming more liked by everyone in the school," start impacting the five people who sit next to you in science class right now. After that, you can start thinking about the entire school. After all, if the entire school is going to like you, that includes those five people in Biology 101.

CHAPTER 5

IF YOU CAN'T BE YOURSELF, BE SOMEBODY ELSE

In fourth grade I was asked to play the role of a king whose wife couldn't cook. I was a good actor and looked pretty fine with a fake beard and crown, if I say so myself. A quiet girl was cast as my culinary-challenged wife. I whined to the teacher that there was no way I could act alongside someone so shy. I knew she'd be a failure. I don't think I'd ever heard this girl say more than three words.

However, as soon as we started practicing our lines, she seemed to become possessed by some outgoing spirit. From start to finish, she belted out her lines with great confidence and played the role of the funny, confident, and outgoing queen with grace and poise. Her performance during the school assembly was electrifying. Afterward, I went up to offer her a word of congratulations and she timidly extended her hand, but said nothing in reply. I don't think I heard three more words before she moved away a few years later.

As mentioned in Chapter 3, whether you are consciously aware of it or not, you are defined by years of brain wiring. Some of this could be positive, like your brain telling you that you're smart. But, you may also have a lot of baggage relating to social situations. You know what I'm talking about, since we all have stories of when someone put us down or rejected us. Most people are bogged down by years of negative self talk, which their brain seems to bring up at the worst possible times (like when you're out on a first date).

You don't have to be handicapped by your faulty brain wiring. And, you don't have to wait years for your new habits to change your brain. I'm going to share with you a secret we developed with Joshua Wagner: you defeat your negativity by simply not being you. That's right; you just quit being yourself for a while. You create your "avatar," which means you become someone else.

You should already have written down your goals (if not, get on it). Now, I need you to take some time to imagine how you would act, look, think, and, most importantly, feel as your best self; you know, the "you" who has achieved those goals. Take those thoughts and feelings and go with them. You're no longer (fill in your given name), but a new, cool, and popular person who does what he wants. Give this new person (your avatar) a name and make it powerful. Don't share it with anyone else because this is for your inspiration and motivation only.

Whenever you are in a situation where you would normally fail, stop being "you" and morph into your avatar. You may be the type of guy who gets scared around cute girls, but your avatar dates anyone he pleases. You may be afraid to stand up to your jerk science teacher, but your avatar is an outgoing winner who speaks her mind (politely and appropriately, of course), even to intimidating authority figures. You get the point.

You may be thinking that my advice will turn you into a liar or a manipulator, but it doesn't have to (and shouldn't). I don't want you to lie or manipulate to reach your goals because, once you're "found out," you'll be back to where you started. Remember that the more you act like your avatar, the more you become your avatar. After all, these are your goals which you are constantly working towards. Acting like you're confident, popular, and the best-looking guy or girl in the school isn't a lie because that's who you're becoming. You're just speeding up the process a little.

The temptation to lie may come from the details. Resist that temptation. If you work at Burger King, don't tell everyone that you're a supermodel. However, if your avatar is a successful model, then go out and find modeling jobs. Then you can tell others that you're starting small in the modeling business, but you're moving up to bigger and better things. And it's all true.

Every popular person, even a celebrity, has an avatar. You can tell this just by turning on the television. Do you really think Dane Cook is funny all the time or Kim Kardashian looks like a photo-shopped babe first thing in the morning? Of course not! They get into their roles and play up the celebrity aspects of their personalities when it's necessary. You should do this too.

Right now your real self and your avatar may be miles apart, but that can change quickly by getting out and living like your avatar. If you find it tough, think about the WWJD bands that were a fad about fifteen years ago. They stood for "What Would Jesus Do?" and the idea was that in times of temptation a person could see the band and make choices according to a Christian perspective. You can ask yourself something similar to bring out your avatar. When you're in a situation that makes you anxious, and you are unsure about your ability to deal with it, ask yourself, "What would (insert your avatar name here) do?"

A few months ago, I was at a water park and met some awesome people. They really liked me and we hung out for most of the day. However, when they were getting ready to leave, I became nervous and hesitated about asking for their contact information. They were younger than I was, so I worried about rejection. My old mentality was getting the best of me. Finally, I asked myself, "What would my avatar do?" He would certainly get their (and anyone's) number. And, he…I mean I…did.

I want to say what an avatar is *not* so you don't get the wrong idea. It's not your childhood fantasy, superhero dream, or anything unobtainable or utterly impractical. Your avatar is your best self, not a comic book character, pipe dream, or hero from your favorite video game.

I knew an obese, out-of-shape guy who once told everyone his lifelong dream was to be a running-back for the Oakland Raiders. Uh huh. Not a good avatar choice.

Your homework for this chapter has two parts. The first assignment is to craft your avatar. With your goals finished (they'd better be by now), you should have an idea of the person you want to be. Now you're creating a "character" who lives those goals. Write down how your avatar dresses, acts, looks, and talks. Who are his friends? How does she respond in difficult situations? Where does your avatar spend his time?

Next, armed with your descriptions, I want you to go out and live like your avatar for a night. It's best not to try this at school, so go to a coffee shop, mall, or anywhere with lots of people. If being your avatar makes you nervous, then try it out in a part of town where nobody knows you or bring a friend for support. And, when you're there, give yourself permission to act as your avatar. Ask yourself, "What would (insert your avatar name) do?" frequently.

Just do it. If you're a little worried about the results, then give yourself permission to be your best self for a few hours at first. I think you'll find that being your best self is easy and even fun, probably much more fun than spending a night being the "old you."

CHAPTER 6

DON'T BE STUCK UP

When I was eighteen, I traveled to Myrtle Beach with a good friend and his family for a summer vacation. One evening, while we were walking to the car from an amazing seafood buffet, his father noticed that my brother and I didn't smile at a girl we passed. He asked us why and we told him we didn't think she was that pretty. He, a master with women, even at seventy (yes, this is true), told us, "Ugly girls need love too."

At first I was annoyed, but his response helped me learn an important life lesson: don't be stuck up, because, when it comes to being popular, everyone is practice. Sure, it would have been cool of me to smile at that girl, but it actually would've also helped me with something I sucked at when I was eighteen...smiling at girls. That's right, if I couldn't or wouldn't smile at a less than attractive girl hundreds of miles from home, how could I smile at the cute girl at the football game? The answer: I couldn't. And didn't.

For someone wanting to be popular, this is a very important chapter and is closely connected to the previous advice of "do the best now" in Chapter 4. Being popular involves being liked by all kinds of people. Do you think only beautiful people watch Robert Pattinson movies? Not if Facebook fan pages are an indication. Are only supermodels among the throngs of fans wanting to see Justin Bieber? Nope. And if you only won over hot girls and guys, you wouldn't even have enough people liking you to be called popular.

So, everyone you encounter is "practice." Everyone. You treat all people like they're potential new friends or at least acquaintances. That guy at the gym who flexes too much? Get him telling others about how awesome you are. The anxious nerd with the zits who works down at Starbucks? Make her one of your adoring fans. The old woman you see walking at the mall? Let her think you're one of the nicest, coolest teenagers on the planet.

If you do this, you'll truly get what popular people have by definition: fans. And these fans will go to bat for you and help you if necessary. Maybe the dude who spends too much time at the gym has a used car he can give you on the cheap when you turn sixteen. The zit-covered teen at Starbucks? How about giving you the senior discount each time you visit (even though you're really just a senior in high school)? And that little old lady at the mall? Maybe she'll think of you when her cute granddaughter or grandson needs a date for the prom.

Now I bet I've gotten your attention.

When everyone is practice, you win big. Besides, as Brian Stepanek knows, becoming popular begins with the number "one." Unless you have a break-out album or are a very, very (very) talented athlete, you have to put in the effort to meet new people and get them to like you. You do that by making sure everyone is practice. This means you talk to the girl who's eating alone at the lunch table before someone else sits down. You invite the new guy at school to go with you to the basketball game before anyone else has even learned his name. And so on.

Your assignment for this chapter is simple. Tomorrow I want you to try to interact in some way with nearly everyone you encounter. You don't have to talk to *everyone* you see because that could be a little creepy. But, you should at least smile or say "hi" to the people who pass in your general direction. And, I want you to really talk to at least five new people. Start doing some of this at school. Eventually, you'll have to introduce your peers to the new you and it's best to start slowly.

Remember to treat everyone the same. Don't let the football player scare you off, or thumb your nose at the elderly sub covering for your science teacher. She might have a hot granddaughter or grandson, remember??

CHAPTER 7

NO ONE IS "OUT OF YOUR LEAGUE"

My sophomore year in high school, through a somewhat chance encounter, I met a very beautiful and popular girl that I had previously only known by reputation. She joined my circle of friends and was really fun to hang out with. Naturally, I had a big crush on her. Although I was pretty popular and it was obvious that she liked me, I still regarded her as "out of my league."

That mentality subconsciously (and even consciously) hampered my efforts at asking her out on a date. After a few weeks, since I had failed to man-up, a good friend ended up asking her out. I thought she'd refuse since I considered her even more out of his league than mine. But, she said "yes" and they ended up dating for several years. I still look back and can't believe what an idiot I was.

You can see other people in two ways. The first is the "leagues" view that I believed: people are categorized into levels, from easily obtainable to "out of my league" (for example, "That guy's tall and handsome; he won't want to be my friend," or "That pretty girl would never date me").

This view creates a pecking order and implies that popular, successful, and beautiful people are somehow radically different from the rest of us. We put them on a pedestal and consider ourselves unworthy to associate with them. This is the common position and it will keep you from being a happy person. Trust me.

The second view sees others in terms of "types." People can be in preferred or non-preferred categories (nerd, jock, hippie, religious, etc.) and you may prefer one to another for friendship, dating, study partner, etc. But, with the "types" perspective, no people are off limits simply because they are too beautiful, too cool, or too anything. This is how successful and popular individuals view the world.

Think about the issue for a minute. A person can live in a trailer with no money to his name and still be a jerk and a snob who wants nothing to do with you. On the other hand, the rich kid in the gated community may be a genuinely amazing guy who wants to be your friend. So, by thinking in terms of leagues, you limit your social interactions, so you will never be popular. However, looking at people in terms of types makes you in charge of your destiny, because you don't preemptively reject a potential friend because of his or her status.

Of course, I also want you to be realistic. Some people will be harder to win over and less available than others. A busy model or actress obviously isn't going to have the free time that your video game playing neighbor has. And, meeting her could be next to impossible. However, that actress still may be a cool and open person you can win over with your skills, if the opportunity arises. And, imagine the reward of winning over someone that popular!

Most people would kill their chances in the beginning by not even trying. While we all may not have the chance to approach models and actresses, the same rule applies to the captain of the football team or the cute girl down the street. They are just another type of person you can (sorry, I mean *will*) impress, not an unapproachable god or goddess who's out of your league.

If it makes you feel better, many people at the top, whether at school or in Hollywood, didn't start out that way and are actually pretty cool. They became popular because they were excellent at relating to people. I've hung out with some very high-society people and I can say with complete honesty that the vast majority are nice, friendly, and cool. There were no more jerks in that group than among the middle class people I knew in high school and still largely associate with today.

Granted, some people made it to the top because they were ruthless and played the game better than anyone else. These guys and girls may not be fun to deal with, but they're also not out of anyone's league. They're just a bigger challenge. Besides even that stuck up, unapproachable snob in your English class has bad breath first thing in the morning and her own share of problems. But, it's probably not a good idea to tell her that until you at least become her friend.

However, don't use thinking of people in terms of "types" to limit yourself either. Never approaching certain "types" due to the challenges they present is just an example of making excuses. A client once told me he doesn't like the hot, confident "type" of woman because she is "too hard to date." Uh huh. That's just "league" thinking using "type" words.

Also, don't get so caught up in putting people into types that you close yourself off to a diverse group of people. For example, avoid saying, "I don't date nerds" or "I can't stand preppy people." You may find the love of your life or your new best friend among the preps or the nerds. It's not just a cliché; opposites often attract for both friendship and dating.

It's going to take a little while to get used to thinking differently about people. We are pretty used to creating a little pyramid in our minds. However, you know better. And the "types" way of thinking gives you access to anyone and everyone, whatever his or her position on the supposed hierarchy. It's what makes you popular. Someone who only gets a certain type of person liking him is the head of a clique and is not truly popular.

Your assignment for this chapter is to believe that there are types, not leagues. But, before you get off too easily, I want you to go out to a social event, party, the mall, or somewhere else busy, and find a person that, if you believed in hierarchies (and you don't), would be the most intimidating person in the place. I want you to go and talk to that guy or girl. Just be friendly and start a conversation. You probably shouldn't try this at your school. Make it someone who doesn't know you just yet.

I want you to notice a couple things. One, the person you chose really is a human being, just like you. He or she may actually be pretty cool. Two, even if that person isn't interested in you, it's not the end of your world to find out that fact. However, you could even make a new friend from this activity. You're popular now. Don't doubt yourself. Just don't blow it like I did all those years ago by not even trying.

CHAPTER 8

VALUE YOUR VALUES

Tim Tebow is a strong evangelical Christian. He's never been quiet about his faith, whether as a college quarterback for the Florida Gators or playing for the Denver Broncos (and later the New York Jets) in the NFL. Tebow is controversial for sure, but there's no doubt that he's popular. Even those who disagree with him typically respect his athleticism. Sure he has haters, but he has many more people who absolutely love him. His jersey sales were number one before he even took a snap as a rookie (2). He's a classic example of how you can stand up for your values and still be popular.

You may already have found this book a little confusing. I talk about being your best self, positively impacting all the people you can, and even brain wiring. This may not sound anything like popularity as you've seen it. Perhaps your experience with popularity is being bullied by the mean girls on the bus, or staring into water as a senior football player shoves your head in the toilet.

This is a legitimate concern. The high school popularity scene can be pretty brutal. However, are those people who bully others or act like jerks *really* popular?

I went to high school with a guy who was pretty good-looking and played multiple sports. He also threatened others all the time. He claimed to be popular and others talked about him like he was popular. But, no one liked him! I'm not even sure what he does for a living today, but since he's pretty much invisible, even locally where I grew up, I'm assuming he's not doing anything worthwhile. Without threats of force, no one wanted anything to do with him. This could be the case with people you know who are supposedly popular, but total jerks.

I am concerned with creating popular, fun, and cool people, not arrogant bullies. The most popular people throughout history are those who bless others with their talents and, in some way, give back to the community. All you have to do is look at the surveys of the most admired people. Every year, they consistently include Mother Teresa, Martin Luther King, Jr., Gandhi, and even Ronald Reagan and Oprah Winfrey. These people all had (or have) values and changed the world for the better. They were not only popular and loved, but very influential.

For example, Martin Luther King, Jr. almost single-handedly improved race relations in the United States. In two hundred years (probably even in two years) no one will remember the mean girl on your bus or the thug in the bathroom (unless they get their acts together).

Perhaps you just want to be famous in a "reality TV" kind of way. If so, you wouldn't be alone and you probably don't need this chapter or even this book. A show like *16 and Pregnant* proves even dumb choices can get you a little bit of fame. Remember, serial killers become famous and make the news. However, they're certainly not popular in a positive sense.

If you want to be popular for a lifetime and impact people inside your school and beyond, then you will need to have ethics. While, I'm not going to go into a deep moral philosophy of popularity, I want to address a few basic ethical guidelines for being popular and still having values.

The first ethical rule of being popular is to simply follow your own value system. Unless you were raised by wolves, you should have a basic set of values. Follow them and don't sell out to be popular. If you are a strong Christian, then find a way to be popular while staying true to your faith. If you love ballet, then don't feel you have to give it up just because all of the supposedly cool girls do another activity.

If you have strong convictions and values, don't change them for the sake of getting others to like you. However, don't be arrogant and use your values to judge others either. If you can stay true to your values and still treat other people right, you will be universally admired for both your excellence and coolness.

The second rule is to leave others better off after meeting you. Chances are you've met someone at least somewhat famous. If the celebrity was cool and gave you some attention back, I'll bet you were happy for hours, maybe even days, after the event. Maybe you still haven't washed the hand that the famous person shook. This is what you should aim for when meeting other people: making them feel better about themselves and giving them a great day.

The third rule is to include, rather than exclude. A truly popular person is always looking to have even more friends and admirers. You don't want to mock others, be a bully, or do something that would otherwise make people hate you. I knew a guy who was really popular with his very small crowd in junior high, but his bullying made sure he was hated by the other ninety percent of the school. You can stand up for yourself and assert your opinions in ways that don't alienate others (see Chapter 27).

If ever in doubt, a good guideline for popular behavior is the "golden rule" given by Jesus: do unto others as you would have them do unto you (i.e. treat others the way you would like to be treated).

Most of us act according to a different rule: do to others what they do to you (or do to them before they do to you). So, by that reasoning, if someone treats you like crap, then you repay the favor and treat them like crap in return. With the golden rule, however, you treat the other person positively. Whatever happens, whether at school, home, or somewhere else, think about how you wished others treated you and act on that rather than continuing the drama or finding creative ways to be a jerk. To put it in modern terms, be cool (see Chapter 18)

For this chapter's homework, I'd like you to write down a list of your core values and reflect on how these will help you or hinder you in becoming popular. Think about how your values can be assets that can make you even more popular. For example, The Killers, a famous pop band, used their Mormon connections to help their career because the lead singer, Brandon Flowers, was (and is) a Mormon. Like Brandon Flowers (and Tim Tebow), you can use your values and your connections to become popular, without having to sell out in the process.

CHAPTER 9

SURVIVAL THROUGH FLEXIBILITY

During the 2011 season of the TV show *Celebrity Apprentice*, country musician John Rich was a finalist, along with actress Marlee Matlin. Rich had scheduled a concert with 80s rock band Def Leppard to promote his business project. On the day of the concert, he went in front of the rather large crowd and announced the coming of Def Leppard to great fanfare and cheers. He was greeted by an empty stage and a clueless looking roadie telling him he got the time wrong. Oops.

What would you have done in John Rich's situation? Would you have totally given up, accepting defeat and humiliation? Or, would you have melted down, showing the world how poorly you perform under pressure? Don't feel bad if you answered "yes" to either (or maybe both) of these questions. It's hard to be calm and relaxed when everything you've planned for and practiced for months or years goes down the toilet. However, if you want to be successful, you have to be flexible and adaptable in every situation.

How does this relate to popularity? Think back to science class. The ability to adapt is the foundation for all life. As you know, every species that failed to adapt throughout history became…well…history. If there's one place that "survival of the fittest" is still alive and well, it's in the American high school. Being popular in high school, heck, even surviving high school, requires a lot of adaptation.

Being mentally and behaviorally flexible means having a good and sensible goal in mind, such as being popular. It also involves being open to using multiple strategies to reach that goal. This means you are willing to try different strategies to reach a goal, keeping the strategies that work, and discarding those that don't. Flexible people know how to respond in a variety of ways to challenging situations, and thus are very successful in life.

To develop flexibility, you will have to relax, stop taking yourself so seriously, and be open to trying new things. The people who have the hardest time adapting are uptight, rigid, and afraid of new ideas. I'm always amazed how people will stubbornly hold to unhelpful ideas, viewpoints, strategies, and images of themselves, even when it is clear these unhelpful ways of thinking and acting are preventing them from achieving their goals.

One great example of an unhelpful strategy rigid people often use is yelling at others. Can you name one time you positively responded to being screamed at? Even though angrily ripping someone doesn't persuade anybody of anything in the long run, most people aren't flexible enough to try another strategy. So all they can do is yell, even if another tactic, such as calm and intelligent discussion, would work so much better to achieve their goal of getting their point across.

If you are naturally a little rigid and want to be more flexible, try to make your everyday choices in the way an adaptable person would. If the cafeteria is out of your favorite food, remember a flexible person will order something else, not throw a fit in front of the lunch lady (which is really attractive, right?).

If your friend can't go out on Saturday because he has to help his dad, don't pout about it. Instead, call someone else. I think you get the idea. An easy way to learn flexibility is to find someone you know who is laid back and flexible. Maybe it's a teacher or a friend. Observe that individual and see how he or she reacts in stressful situations. I always found it amusing when my students would come to me without their homework, nearly having a nervous breakdown. I'd usually say, "Give it to me tomorrow." Yes, I'm pretty flexible.

If you are serious about being popular, you must always be ready to adapt, especially in social situations. I'm sure you know how quickly trends change. When I was a teen, it was popular for guys to part their hair in the middle and let it hang off the sides of their forehead. Guys who had that haircut were soooo cool. If I was your teacher with a haircut like that, what would you do? You'd probably laugh me out of the classroom, thinking I was clueless. And, I'd deserve it. However, some people who lived in the mid-1990s *still* have their hair that way.

It's not just keeping up with styles and trends that will require flexibility. Think about how often conversations, situations, and circumstances change. Maybe you were counting on making the cheerleading squad to be cool. You get cut. Then what? Or perhaps you wanted to ask the pretty freshman girl out to Homecoming, but on your chosen day you have a giant zit on your forehead. What now? In these and every scenario, you survive and thrive because you can think on your feet and adapt.

Also, other kids will be watching you to see what happens when you experience challenges. It's a sad fact life, but there are petty people who will actually be happy when you fail. Look at how we treat our celebrities. If you're popular, even in high school, you will have to expect some of it too.

When I was a teen, a mean teacher had his fly unzipped and the students had a field day with laughter. Fortunately, one cool and courageous guy told him about it. However, many others were happy to see him humiliated. This teacher, to his credit, laughed it off. He was, in that situation, flexible enough not to get bothered by it. Hardly anyone even brought it up again. Flexibility like this ensures that there will never really be true failure (more on this in Chapter 11).

By the way, this teacher wasn't the only good example of flexibility. Remember my story of John Rich? In what had to be a truly embarrassing and stressful moment, he didn't even show the world he was bothered. He apologized for the mix-up, borrowed a guitar from the roadie, and started performing his own songs.

John Rich became the warm-up act for Def Leppard. Because of his flexibility, the audience was able to hear two famous artists that night. Not only that, but he probably went away with thousands of new fans, especially after the episode aired on television.

John Rich's flexibility should be a good model for you. He didn't melt down. He didn't freak out. He calmly adapted and turned what could be a very bad situation into a scenario that earned him respect and more fans.

Your assignment is to add being flexible and adaptable to your goals and declarations. I challenge you to make being flexible a priority in your life, even if it means becoming more open to new ways of thinking and acting. You may have to work hard to change your old (and possibly rigid) ways of doing things, but it's absolutely worth it to become a more flexible person. High School is really dramatic and the only way to stay above it is to be flexible and open.

Next, you'll need to go out and practice your new, flexible perspective on a daily basis. If you are naturally uptight, this is essential. However, even those of us who are pretty flexible sometimes need a reminder in stressful situations. If you ever have trouble being flexible and adaptable, here's my best advice: laugh at yourself when you get too rigid. It almost always works.

CHAPTER 10

GIVE-GET-GIVE (THEN GET SOME MORE)

The Oscars, and many other award shows, hand out gift baskets to the celebrity presenters. Some of these gift bags are worth more than ten thousand dollars! You may be thinking: ten thousand dollars? For already wealthy people? What's up with that? I used to think that too. I didn't understand why anyone would give freebies to famous millionaires. After all, these guys can afford anything they want.

But, now that I am popular and teach popularity to others, it all makes sense. Although celebrities and other successful people are usually wealthy, they don't just take money and attention from others. They also give something valuable to the world. And, of course, the more they give, the more they get from others. "Give-get-give" is an endless circle that makes people popular, successful, and in many cases, rich.

Let me give you a fictional, but possible, example of the "give-get-give" philosophy in action using the celebrity gift bag. Let's say a clothing company gives Miranda Cosgrove a few shirts that would sell for two hundred dollars in the store (the company gives). Perhaps she, out of gratitude or as a part of a deal, wears the shirt in public and other young people want to buy the shirt (the company gets). Then, maybe the company decides that since she has been such a good marketer for them, they offer her an endorsement deal (they give). Then, the cycle begins again and they make a lot of money. You can see why people give free stuff to celebrities now.

However, "give-get-give" is not just a celebrity phenomenon. Like many of the tips in this book, it's also a trait of very successful people. Let's look at successful businesspeople, athletes, and musicians. They don't become wealthy because people randomly give away money. No, these famous people give others something they want, like a gadget, service, or even entertainment. Kobe Bryant wouldn't be popular if he was a shoe salesman. But, because he gives people excitement and entertainment, he's rich and popular.

You can also see the "give-get-give" principle in action at your high school. Who are the most popular kids at your school? If you have the companion workbook, write down their names. Now, think about what they give to others to be popular. Maybe they're talented at sports and make the student body feel proud at sporting events. Perhaps they are physically beautiful, which is also a highly valued trait. Or it could be they have a sense of humor or acting ability.

The people you listed are popular because they offer something of value to others. They give and they, in return, get attention, love, fame, etc. Then, they give to larger numbers of people and get even more attention. People have a strong urge to give back when they've received something. It's called reciprocity.

Let's look at another example: the star football player helps the school win and the guy at IHOP, who went to the school and played football himself, might, out of gratitude, give the guy a free meal. It doesn't seem fair, but it's the way life works. If you aren't popular, you may need to ask what you're giving your classmates, family, and friends. Chances are, you're not giving them something they value, if anything at all.

One summer, while traveling, I went to a Caribou Coffee I'd never visited before. I walked in with my brother and we started some of our humor routines (see Chapter 14). After interacting with the cashier for a little while (and getting a free iced coffee), she told us that we made her day because, get this, she NEVER encounters people like us. We made her laugh during a boring and frustrating day and we got a free coffee out of the deal. I would argue, however, that she got more value. A good day is worth far more than a two-dollar coffee. But, because she was a barista by trade, coffee was what she had to give. So, she gave it.

Getting in the "give-get-give" mindset can be tough. We're used to thinking in terms of scarcity. In other words, we think we can't give something away because we're afraid we won't get anything in return. So, we become cheap with money and time and aren't generous to others for fear of being taken advantage of. Maybe you shared a talent once and got laughed at or perhaps you tried out for a team and got cut. Now, you are scared of giving to the world because you think no one will give you anything (like popularity) in return. That attitude will have to go.

Every day is like Christmas when you "give-get-give."

Give of your best self all the time and be generous with your money, time, and talents. If you follow the advice in this book, you can give of yourself and people will actually just want to be around you. Seriously. If you can reach lots of people with your talents, you'll be popular for sure.

Look at Google. They give away the vast, vast majority of their services, yet make more money than most other companies on the planet. Their "give-get-give" mindset has made their owners billionaires. I guarantee that if Google charged for all their services, they probably wouldn't even be around today. They give freely to others and those "others," when they are willing to pay for services (like advertising), choose Google over their competitors.

A great example of someone who gives of himself is friend and athlete Roy W. Hall. A wide receiver with the Ohio State Buckeyes and then the Indianapolis Colts and Detroit Lions, Hall has certainly had a good taste of fame and celebrity, especially since he was a part of the National Championship Ohio State team in 2002.

Roy gave of his talents to the Ohio State Buckeyes in a sport that requires lots of time, practice, and bodily abuse. The OSU fans, in return for his hard work and success, gave him their love, support, and admiration. After he retired from the NFL, Roy, a smart, articulate, and passionate guy dedicated to his family and his faith, started giving back to the Columbus community through his non-profit D.R.I.V.E.N. Foundation.

D.R.I.V.E.N. provides educational programming along with support services to underserved communities throughout Central Ohio and surrounding cities. His charity work not only helps disadvantaged individuals, but also increases his networking contacts and impact on the community. Thus, he continues to "get" new opportunities as well. He is a perfect example of "give-get-give" at work. Incidentally, if you want to be generous with your money and/or time, you can support D.R.I.V.E.N. by going to http://drivenfoundation.org or by following Roy on Twitter under the username @Roy_Hall.

The hardest part of give-get-give is to take that first step and actually give. When we have something of value, it's very tough to give it away. However, with time, ideas, and talents it's absolutely essential that we share them with the world if we ever want to see anything (like money, fame, or popularity) given to us in return.

Your homework for this chapter, if you haven't already done it, is to list popular people in your school as well as why they are popular. After that, list your talents and think of ways you can give these talents to the world. Don't worry about how you're going to "get" anything in return at this stage. If you have something genuine to offer the world and give it abundantly, you will receive more back than you know what to do with. If you can't think of a talent, then see Chapter 13. Someday there may even be a celebrity gift bag with your name on it.

Chapter 11

There's No Failure, Only Feedback

When I was in eighth grade, we were forced to take home economics, which basically involved cooking and sewing. I hated it until I found out that we were going to make donuts, which excited my chubby, teen self. To make these treats, we were organized into groups and each member was put in charge of one aspect of donut making. The process went well until my group leader poured the donut batter into the fryer. Instead of keeping a nice, rounded shape, the "donuts" looked like deep-fried splattered mud.

When the teacher came by, she asked us what happened and I had no idea. It turns out that one of my cooking partners, God bless her, hadn't correctly measured the sugar. As we stared at the gooey mess in the deep fryer with dejected faces, the teacher didn't yell at us. She just asked if we learned from our mistake. We answered in the affirmative.

Next time, not only would Sarah measure correctly, but as a team, we would look out for each other.

When the teacher gave us our team grade a few days later, I fully expected to fail. Obviously, the purpose of the project was to make donuts and we simply made deep-fried brown sludge. However, we ended up getting an A-. I was shocked. The teacher noted on the grading rubric that we received a good grade because while other people had made decent donuts, we actually learned a valuable cooking (and life) lesson. And, we did.

A popular and successful person doesn't have the word "failure" in his or her vocabulary. History is filled with people who had setback after setback, but still ultimately succeeded in their final goals. A classic example is Abraham Lincoln who lost several major elections before ultimately winning the presidency twice. Lincoln could've just given up, but instead, he kept trying until he eventually achieved the highest elected office in the United States.

I have a lot of faith in my techniques. They've worked for me and they've worked for many friends and clients. However, every tip isn't going to work all the time. And, even if the methods are great, it doesn't mean you'll execute them perfectly. Not only that, but even the most successful people have their off days (even the best baseball hitters of all time still get an "out" six of ten at bats). What this means is that you will experience setbacks. You will fall flat on your face. You will experience rejection. You will experience what others call "failure."

When you experience a setback, you have two options. The first is to let the lack of success cripple you. You can do this by:

1. Dwelling on it and getting depressed over it.

2. Claiming it is someone else's fault, when it was yours.

3. Believing, in spite of the evidence, it was actually a success.

I've seen all of these at work in my teaching experience. I've known students who've dwelt so long and hard on one particular setback that it emotionally destroyed them. For example, I heard many kids say, "I can't do math" because they once struggled in a math class. The "blame game" was also popular, especially if I caught someone cheating. Many of them got caught again by other teachers because it was always "someone else's" fault.

Finally, I've watched others continue on ineffective paths when all evidence says it's time to change. Ironically, this problem mostly occurred with my teaching colleagues who couldn't adapt when their teaching methods were obviously failing. What worked in the 1970s isn't necessarily effective in the 2010s. But, change was just too hard.

The second option is to actually learn from your "failure." When you learn from your mistakes through feedback, you don't even really experience failure. Take a football player who gets benched for poor performance. He can sulk and pout or he can receive feedback from his coaches and practice like crazy. Chances are if he listens and practices, he will be back on the field in no time and be a better player than ever. In this scenario, his benching wasn't a failure, but a great opportunity to actually become better.

As far as your situation goes, you know the problems associated with surviving as a teenager in the twenty-first century. When I was in high school, if someone messed up or said something stupid, it was usually confined to a small group. With the internet, social media, and texting, our stupid moments can be broadcast for all to see within seconds and may be out on the web forever! You have potential to not only "fail," but fail big time.

While you have to be on the lookout for problems and issues and avoid them (always think before you act and be responsible), you'll also have to view setbacks as opportunities to learn from your mistakes. For example, there are teens who have sent dirty pictures of themselves to another person and the pictures were then distributed around the whole school. While someone who does this will have to deal with the consequences, that person can learn from the mistake by resolving to act in a way that preserves his or her dignity in the future. That kind of life change will at least make sure the individual in question never has to undergo that type of humiliation in the future.

Right now I'd like you to make a list of major "failures" in your life. Maybe it was a rejection in seventh grade, a failed class, or a decision that got you grounded or humiliated. This activity may be painful, but it's important to complete. For each mistake you've listed, I want you to come up with a couple of lessons that you've learned. If you haven't really learned a lesson from a major setback, then I urge you to think long and hard about it now and come up with some. You definitely don't want to go down an unsuccessful path more than once.

However, you also don't want to dwell on your previous mistakes to the point that you are crippled by your past. Almost all successful people are like Abraham Lincoln. They've had an election, project, album, job, movie, or incident they wish they could forget. However, that didn't stop them from being successful. You should always learn from your mistakes, but don't focus too much on the mistakes themselves.

This is Chapter 11 for a reason (Google it). Learn from your mistakes, then start over. With everything in life, there is no failure, only feedback (at least if you make it that way).

CHAPTER 12

LET GO AND CHILL OUT

On one episode of the 1980s television show *The Wonder Years* which takes place in the late 1960s and early 1970s, the lead character, teenager Kevin Arnold, walks into baseball practice. Even though he isn't on the team, he steps up to bat. He hits a home run. The coaches eagerly put him on the team, but he struggles, barely getting another hit, let alone a home run. Eventually he gets cut, but guess what happens when he steps up to the plate for one last swing before exiting the baseball field? He hits a home run!

This story illustrates the importance of detachment. Detachment is doing what you know to be excellent, but not caring about any particular outcome. An "outcome" could be a spot on the team, being friends with someone, getting money, or anything that we desire. Detachment is considered a sign of enlightenment in many of the world's religions, probably because experience shows that many of the best things in life happen to people who are detached. Or, to put it in teenage language, detachment means to do what you know is best (this book is helping you with this) at every step and not get worked up about what does or doesn't come at the end.

The opposite of detachment is attachment. Attachment is when we cling to outcomes, positions, emotions, substances, or even people. Not all attachment is bad, but being too attached to anything can certainly cloud our minds.

In my work with addicts, I've seen a lot of attachment. People are so attached to a chemical, that it quite literally takes over their lives to the point that everything they do is oriented towards finding a drug. Being overly attached to anything, even good things like love, severely limits our flexibility and can cause problems. For example, it's good to be attached to our parents. But, if we're so dependent on our parents that we need them to come on dates with us, that's bad!

You may have examples from your life of failing when you were attached, yet succeeding when you simply didn't care. That's detachment at work. I had friends who tried for years to have a child, desperately hoping for the woman to get pregnant. After several years, they gave up and adopted. What happened a couple months later? She got pregnant. Believe it or not, these stories are common and three to ten percent of adopting couples get pregnant after the adoption (3).

I'm not going to try to figure out the mind of God or the exact science behind it, but, for whatever reason, good things happen when we detach, but when we're desperately attached, we don't get our way. Maybe when we detach we align our will with God's purposes or the laws of Universe. Or, maybe on a more earthly level, we are our best, relaxed selves when we stop being so uptight and hung up on a particular outcome.

Detachment is a general success and spiritual principle, but it's also vitally important if you want to be popular. In many cases, the most popular people in any environment are the most relaxed. This doesn't mean they don't care or are lazy. Far from it. They work hard and have a lot of passion. But, they don't need the outcome, so they appear much more attractive. It's why someone who has a bunch of friends gets even more, but the desperate and friendless dude can't seem to catch a break.

Let's take an example of well-known celebrities. It can be any of them. Pick one. They've been on television, made movies, and make more money than the gross national product of some small countries. What outcome could they be attached to? None! They can go through life totally in the moment and let their true selves shine through. They have to impress no one. I don't know any mega celebrities personally, so I'm not saying all of them live detached lives, but they certainly could.

As you practice the techniques to be popular, detachment will be a huge part of your success. You'll be approaching random people, getting phone numbers, using new forms of humor, making bold and independent moves, and even experiencing setbacks on many occasions. These are not easy tasks. In fact, just mentioning them may be making you a little sick to your stomach! That's all normal. But, it means you'll have to relax. You will have to make "it doesn't matter" your catchphrase when doing the difficult tasks this book recommends. The girl turns you down when you ask her to homecoming? It doesn't matter. No one laughs when you tell a joke? It doesn't matter. You trip and fall in front of a popular girl? It doesn't matter.

Detachment, as I mentioned earlier, is considered a pretty advanced spiritual technique. In some religions, it's even regarded as a sign of enlightenment. Nonetheless, I'm going to try to teach you a little bit about being detached. You may not become a saint or the fifteenth Dalai Lama, but my advice should be good enough to at least help you become popular and maybe even a better human being.

First, you need to keep everything in perspective. Remember the importance of perspective? That hasn't decreased in importance since the second chapter. The right perspective is this: you can recover from anything short of death. So, the "it doesn't matter" thing? If you're not six feet under, it's always true. Life is a gift and as long as your heart is beating you have a second chance.

Let's take a deeper look at my earlier examples. A girl turns you down for Homecoming? Is it really that big of a deal in the grand scheme of things? Fifteen years later I can barely remember the girl I went *with* to Homecoming, let alone who turned me down. No one laughs at your joke? Who cares? In a minute, they'll have forgotten all about you and your bomb. The popular girl sees you fall? If you laugh it off, she may think you're cool and even talk to you to make sure you're okay. Even if she doesn't, who cares? Does one fall seen by one girl set the tone for your entire life? It sure shouldn't.

Second, practice mindfulness. A concept that is promoted by most of the world's religions to some degree or another, mindfulness is paying attention in the present moment non-judgmentally. You aren't burdened by your past and you don't worry about the future. You take in the smells, the sounds, the sights, and above all, the feeling of your surroundings. You make the journey just as important as the destination. You pay attention (see Chapter 25).

You've probably been told throughout your life not to live in the moment, but to always think about your future. And, if the moment involves doing drugs or harming yourself and others, it's true. However, we've so internalized the "don't live in the moment" mindset, that most of us spend all our present moments thinking about something else. Let me give you an example. If you sit quietly for about five minutes right now, I'll bet something negative enters your mind related to the past or the future. It could be your failure to answer a question correctly in science class earlier today, or the dentist appointment you have next Tuesday.

Look at all the people who constantly dwell on the past. They are crippled by long-gone relationships or held down by something they were told when they were five. Their present is held hostage by events that ended long ago. The same is true, however, of those who worry about the future. They stress about failing tests, not making the winning catch, and any number of "what if" scenarios that make the present miserable as they constantly worry about what possibly, maybe, might happen. Mindfulness is the perfect antidote.

If you're not in your bedroom, think of it right now. What designs are on the carpet? What does the texture of the ceiling look like? What is the shape of the woodwork or the trim? If you're in your room now, ask these questions of your family's kitchen. Can you answer these questions? If you can't, you're not all that different from most people. After all, you just live there; you don't actually pay attention to it.

If you want to be popular and successful, you'll need to make mindfulness a priority. If you find yourself moving too quickly and becoming too focused on an outcome, take a step back and enjoy the little moments of life. If in doubt, just stop and take in everything your senses can handle. Smell. See. Taste. Touch. Listen. Mindfulness is simply observing the present moment in a non-judgmental way. Don't analyze the moment; just enjoy it.

Notice how life slows down and your anxiety disappears. You see, this is why detachment is important for being popular. Mindful people are cool, calm, and relaxed (see Chapter 18). They're the type of people everyone wants as friends. You can hang out with them and date them and know you're always in for a good, fun, stress-free time. Popularity is a great thing and it may be something you want desperately. However, you can't let that desperation or that desire to be popular run (or ruin) your life.

Third, detachment requires flexibility (see Chapter 9). There are many, many ways to get to an outcome. Just because you have a particular path to a goal in your head doesn't make it the correct or even preferred method of achieving it. If a path towards your outcome doesn't seem to be working due to your own fault or an outside circumstance, then take another.

Stress kills. Deal with it in the right way.

The road to success often takes unique and surprising turns for many people. Don't give up on your dreams, but be flexible enough to see the many roads that could take you there. Even supposed setbacks could be blessings in disguise…if you're flexible enough to adapt and grow from them.

Finally, meditate a little bit. I'm not trying to convert you to any religion, just asking you to give a few minutes a day to relax, be mindful, and experience some needed down-time. I knew a girl who went to school, studied for two hours, then had practice and games for two volleyball leagues! Does this sound like you? Maybe you just sit around and do nothing all day. Well, this isn't really relaxation either, just boredom. If you're like most modern teenagers, you could use some relaxation or at least a break from family, friends, school or other stressors. Find a silent space and just take it easy. You can just sit and reflect, pray, or even say your affirmations/goals.

Whatever method you choose, the most important point of meditation is to give some quality time each day to yourself. I've never once wished I had spent my meditation time doing something else. Each and every time I've meditated, even if it was for five minutes, I've felt mentally more powerful and less stressed the entire day. So, even if you're extremely busy, make meditation a priority. Five minutes of meditation a day will make the remaining twenty-three hours and fifty-five minutes much more meaningful.

But, don't let meditation stress you out. Some people think meditation has to be done in a lotus position in total silence in the middle of the woods. While this may be cool, it's unrealistic for most people and they end up feeling stressed about not meditating "properly." Meditation could be five minutes with your head down at study hall or ten minutes quietly listening to music in your bedroom. If it relaxes you and releases stress, do it.

Tonight, take five minutes and meditate before bed. When you wake up tomorrow, do it again before you leave for school. If you can meditate longer, then keep going until you either want to stop or your schedule demands it. If you're not alone in your house, let everyone know to leave you alone. Turn off your cell phone and cover each visible clock. If you need to stop at a certain time, set an alarm, but still cover the clock, so you can remain in the present moment.

You may be laughing and asking, "Why the effort? It's only five minutes!" Can you stay focused for five whole minutes? In the age of text messages, the internet, and instant social media, don't be so sure. I've been meditating for years and still have focus issues. You may be a natural, but for the rest of us, I advise starting small and removing all distractions. In fact, most meditation experts suggest starting the practice by paying complete attention to *three* full breaths. That isn't a misprint...most people struggle just to do that at first.

Tomorrow, I want you to focus on living in the present all day. Forget about the fears of yesterday and the anxieties of tomorrow, and experience the present. If you find yourself worrying about the future or dwelling on the past, just bring your awareness back to the present moment. Resist the urge to "fight" intrusive thoughts and distractions.

This will only intensify them. I guarantee living mindfully for an entire day will positively impact you and those around you.

Before I wrap up, I should note that it's very easy to get into a habit of worry and stress, especially at a high-pressure place like school. Whenever you start to become stressed, take a deep breath and just let your senses overtake you. In other words, whenever you need it, create a short meditation break when you pay attention to a few breaths and other sensations you feel at that moment. Feel the air enter the tip of your nose, and then become aware of the sensation of the breath entering the lungs and then exiting them. Mindfulness is just that simple.

For more detailed information about mindfulness and meditation techniques, please check out the resources at the end of this book.

These tips may not seem like they're designed to make you popular. However, don't neglect chapters that seem vaguely connected to popularity. They are some of the most important tips because they build a powerful *mental* foundation upon which you will construct the new, popular, you.

CHAPTER 13

BE FUNNY

I have a friend named Jasmine whom I met in high school. She was, to say the least, a little "complicated." She pretty much treated everyone like dirt every single day. She tossed out put-downs to nearly every brave soul who tried to reach out to her. Lots of people tried to break through her emotional wall, but no one succeeded. Except for two guys. Both of them have the last name Bennett and were involved in writing this book.

Jasmine treated David and me with (relative) kindness because, instead of getting angry at her daily tests, we responded with humor and even gave her some of her crap back, but in a funny way. We watched her go from angry to putty in our hands. And, it's all due to a secret power that can influence almost anyone. Sorry if you were expecting a different, more awesome answer, but our secret weapon is pretty ordinary. It's humor.

Laughter has been shown through numerous scientific studies to have major health benefits. It lowers stress, builds up your immune system, and decreases blood pressure. It also releases endorphins, the brain chemicals that make us feel happy (4). In addition, it's hard to be angry, fearful, anxious, or generally negative while laughing. Humor makes us happy and is contagious. It's a great technique to be popular. And, studies show that funny men are rated as more attractive to women than humorless guys.

In spite of the obvious benefits of laughter, most people don't get nearly enough of it. One study showed that children generally laugh three hundred times in one day. This is true of my daughter who is five: she is almost always laughing and smiling. You probably aren't surprised to learn that the average adult laughs only around twenty times a day (5). After all, aren't the adults you know stress free, happy, popular, and successful? Ha!

I believe that the teenage years are when most people become humor challenged. You probably experience this firsthand. Have you ever heard anyone say, "You're in high school now; it's time to start being serious?" Or maybe you heard an adult burst your bubble by crushing your dreams and telling you how hard life is. Not only that, but it's easy for the stress and pain of the teenage years to suck the humor right out of you. If any of this describes you, you're certainly not alone.

However, from my experience, I don't think most teens or adults want such little humor in their lives. It's just the way everyone is expected to act. Some of my teaching colleagues and I were once even told not to joke around with students after school. But, the expectation to always be serious doesn't reduce the actual need for humor in the world. I'd say laughing two to three hundred times a day is probably the right number. In that case, we have a very serious laughter deficit. And, it's making people stressed and miserable and no doubt contributing to many of the health problems plaguing the United States.

The humor deficit isn't all bad news. You can benefit from this humor challenged, yet laughter needy, society by bringing hilarity to the world. In fact, if I had to pick one, and only one, trait that has made me popular, including in my role as a teacher, it would be my humor (I ignored the principal on the "no joking around" thing). If I didn't consistently make people genuinely laugh wherever I go, I would never have become popular and loved like I am today.

However, one of the reasons that more people don't laugh on a regular basis is that not everyone is funny. Delivering jokes and coming up with funny material is a true art and not everyone is close to being blessed with the skills. Browse YouTube videos for ten minutes and that should be very obvious. Also, most would-be comedians simply repeat stale routines from television or the internet hoping no one will ever know they don't have an original bone in their body.

Researchers who have studied humor (yes there are people who pursue this cool area of study) have looked at what makes humor effective. The first aspect of successful humor they discovered is incongruity (6). If something is incongruent, it "doesn't fit." This could be anything from a joke that has no punch line to a picture of a cat wearing sunglasses.

A good example is the British show *Trigger Happy TV* where a couple of the guys in the comedy troupe dress up in cute animal outfits and then "beat up" fellow human cast members in public. It's funny because the image is completely incongruent with our expectations of human-squirrel relations. Nobody expects to see a guy in a squirrel costume wrestling somebody on his way to work either.

It sounds kind of complicated at first, but you can use incongruity to great effect when you talk to other people. It's one of my favorite ways to make people laugh. For example, I use a tip I learned from Joshua Wagner and inject (pardon the pun) drug related humor into the conversation. I'll order a coffee with cream, sweetener, and meth. Most people do a double-take, and then break into laughter. It's very incongruent because number one, it's not a typical coffee order. The incongruity is increased by the fact that I am a total health nut with a fit body, clear skin, and great teeth. If I were a meth junkie, then such a coffee order would be congruent and an occasion for sadness or revulsion, not humor.

Another aspect of successful humor is thinking about unpleasant things from a position of safety. This simply means that the person hearing the joke thinks about something he wouldn't want to happen to him (like getting kicked "you know where") but is not actually experiencing it, which would be painful rather than funny. Laughter probably developed as a way for us to calm ourselves following a stressful event (7). If we were being chased by wooly mammoths, when we finally made it back to the village, away from the stress, the tribe's joker would say something like, "That's nothing. I've been chased by my wife for years. But I've never escaped her yet." Then, everyone laughed, the adrenaline decreased, and the stress of the chase eased.

This is why we find other people getting scared (like when someone jumps out of a closet) funny from the comfort of our living rooms. If a total stranger really were in our closet, it wouldn't be funny at all. Even if it were a joke, in the moment, it would still be scary and we couldn't laugh until we settled down, were safe, and realized it was a joke.

The squirrel beating up the human is a great example of safety as well. Clearly if a giant squirrel were going all MMA on a guy in front of your house, it would be cause for panic. Yet, when you're watching it from the safety of your room on YouTube (and know it's fake), it's quite funny. The same is true of the meth joke. If I were really a meth junkie, the person I'm joking with would really have to be afraid. Yet, with a clean cut guy like me, there is safety.

When using humor at school, parties or in public, you must always think of the safety issue. Just because no one's being chased by a giant squirrel doesn't mean the other person feels safe. The issue of safety is why, I believe, inappropriate humor is hated by large parts of the population. Jokes about race, violence, and sex will take away the feeling of safety for many people because these issues have created a lack of security for them. So, obviously, if you are trying to be popular, you should be very, very careful about using dark or edgy humor, especially around people you don't know. If you cross the line into creepy (see Chapter 24), kiss popularity goodbye.

Another way to be funny is to use situational or observational humor. This is adapting your jokes to current situations. For example, if you are in science class, you would make jokes about the lab, the material, the people in the class, the teacher, etc. This type of humor is perfect because it has to be original and it makes you look intelligent and witty. Situational humor can also be based around current events like what's happening at your school or in the world. It proves that you pay attention and are smart.

Once David and I used a mix of safety, incongruity, and situational humor for great effect with a couple of teenage employees we know at a coffee shop. One asked what was in my briefcase. She knew it was probably a computer and was trying to be funny. I told her my machine gun is in there (it was a computer). She laughed and told me, "Yeah right." I then asked her if she'd heard of the trade in body parts from executed Chinese prisoners in the news. She gave me a horrified look and said "no." I stared at my briefcase and asked, "Know anyone who needs a kidney?" Both girls burst into laughter.

That example shows not only a mix of the three types of humor, but also is a little dark and edgy. It pushes some boundaries and you (or your parents) may not even find it funny at all. However, I knew the girls well enough and delivered the joke in a way to pull it off. Sure, it was a gamble, but it paid off big-time because it made me look smart and very original. In fact, both girls still jokingly ask me if I have any more body parts for sale. When you are trying material, you have to decide if you think an edgier approach is worth the risk. In most cases, it won't be, but you have to be flexible.

Two other types of humor you may want to consider using are anti-humor and the shaggy dog story. I have found both of these very effective in my years of making friends and being popular.

Anti-humor is telling a story or joke that is so clearly unfunny that it ends up being funny. An example is when I go to a restaurant with my brother and ask for something ridiculous, like a coffee with twenty espresso shots. The employees will usually laugh because they sense it's a joke, although they're not totally sure. David, however, will chime in with a straight face: "No, he's serious. He's a late-stage caffeine addict and needs his fix." Almost everyone thinks about it, and then laughs. However, notice there is no joke or punch line

A shaggy dog story is a long and pointless story, usually with ridiculous details and an absurd conclusion. These are even funnier if you deliver them with a straight face. Once when David and I were at a water park, we were telling a guy about how before I lost a bunch of weight I got stuck in one of the slides and they had to use the Jaws of Life to get me out. And I celebrated my rescue with a giant ham dinner. Remember, shaggy dog stories work best with incongruity, so you must make sure that if you're telling an alleged story about yourself, it must be incongruent with your personality. In my example, I was shirtless at a water park, so he could tell I was in great shape. The story was totally BS and the guy knew it. But, for my listener, it was like being sucked into a brief, amusing fantasy.

Another way to make jokes is to understand and play off the multiple meanings of words that people use. This can be very funny if done properly, but avoid being too dorky about it, or the joke won't go over very well.

For example, when David orders fast food and the cashier asks him if he is eating "here" or "to go," he says "here." Then he pauses and says, "Well...not right here...actually over there" as he points to the booth where he will eat. This is playing on the word "here." Since he does it with a confident, yet fake-confused tone, it almost always gets a laugh, because it breaks people's normal expectations of their use of the word. Another example is when we are out together, and a hostess will say, "Are you two together?" She means, "Are you two *dining* together?" David responds by giving a confused look and saying, "Oh no, we're just friends." It gets a laugh because it plays on the word "together."

Another way to do this is to "misunderstand" words or phrases. For example, if someone just told you that they joined the "math club," you could remark that you are amazed a school would even have a *meth* club, and jokingly express your interest in joining that club. This type of humor, even though you're pretending to be dumb, actually makes you appear smart and high-value. See, your English class does have a point.

Just remember, when trying to be humorous, that saying or doing something for shock value alone is rarely funny. In addition, humor is one area where it's possible to be very creepy. Telling jokes about inappropriate topics can have the effect of creeping people out, especially if you generally look and act like a weirdo. I could get away with the Chinese execution joke because I'm a well-dressed professional and the girls knew I was safe. A guy with a bunch of piercings, a mohawk, and black, ripped clothing whom they'd never seen before would probably be more believable than incongruent.

Finally, use your judgment to determine when to be funny. I knew a guy who actually walked into a funeral after a huge tragedy and started joking around with the family. Needless to say, they tossed him out of the church (quite literally) and he lost several friends. Know when it's time to be funny and when to be serious. In spite of this advice, I still believe humor is appropriate in probably ninety-five percent of situations, even if some uptight person thinks otherwise. Still, be aware of the five percent of times when you must be serious.

Finally, I think I should say something about the universal appeal of humor. Some of you may be a little worried taking humor advice from a guy in his thirties. Let me put your mind at ease. Every personal example I've shared from Jasmine to the water park involved teenagers. When I was a teacher, I constantly received positive feedback on student evaluations about being funny, and even today I have people of all ages, teens included, laughing. Good humor will be appreciated by people of all ages, from the teenager to the old lady down the road.

For homework, I'd like you to get on YouTube and watch a few hours of great comedians. I'd recommend successful ones like Chris Rock, Jeff Foxworthy, and Dane Cook. However, you can pick anyone who is popular and universally appreciated.

You can also visit humor websites like Cracked.com. These should give you an idea of how humor works, and how to tell stories, deliver punch-lines, etc. If you know a funny person, then go out and watch him or her in action. Take mental notes and see how he or she gets people to laugh. Finally, begin to think about what types of humor you would be most comfortable using. In the next chapter, you'll start coming up with actual material.

CHAPTER 14

MAKE IT ROUTINE

Watching my good friend and business partner Joshua Wagner in action when we go out in public is a real pleasure. He has a way of making people laugh from the time they meet him until he gets their number or a Facebook friend request. And, he inevitably becomes their friend and sees them again. Why? Because, as mentioned in the last chapter, people's lives are often missing humor and they gladly take the opportunity to make friends with funny people.

Joshua is a naturally funny guy, but, as a stand-up comedian on the side, he knows what you're born with will only get you so far. He has practiced and memorized routines for years. He literally has hours of material that he can pull out any time he needs it. So, there's never a dull moment with him, unless he feels like being dull. Knowing routines makes him the master of the conversation and keeps him the center of attention. That's a large part of being popular, right?

From a comedy standpoint, a routine is just a series of funny stories, lines, jokes, etc. They are not one-off comments or jokes, but sustained attempts at being funny for a longer period of time. The best comedian's routines will effortlessly shift from theme-to-theme and stack jokes, lines, and stories so that the audience remains captivated for the entire show. When you go out and meet new people, you'll want to have enough routines to keep people laughing and enjoying your presence for as long as you're with them.

You have three options with routines: make your own, find someone else's, or a create mixture of the two. I would advise that in the beginning you pick option three and eventually just make your own. I would never recommend using someone else's routines unchanged. They can be very unnatural because they don't reflect your life situation. Not only that, but if you simply repeat memorized material, it will come across too much like pick-up lines. And people hate pick-up lines because the only skill they require is memorizing something that you read on the internet.

To start, find some general humor routines on the internet. You should've already looked up comedians on YouTube, but you can also search for websites that specialize in creating funny routines. Then, practice doing the routines, adapting them to suit your personality and your interests. It's key that if you use other people's material, you change it to fit your situation. I once knew a teenage guy who used a routine based around his allegedly comical failure at dancing lessons. It turns out the girl he tried to impress was a dancer and asked him follow-up questions wanting more detail. When he couldn't deliver he looked like a tool. This guy played football, so he should've adapted the routine to a football story.

Second, you'll have to actually go out and practice the routines. Practice with family and friends first. You'll find out what works and what doesn't in a low-stress environment. View it like an experiment. If a routine doesn't work, then you may have to junk it. If parts of it don't work, then you'll know what to change before going "live." If you're brave, you can practice in public, but I'd still avoid practicing at school at this point. Wait until you've at least mastered some material first.

After some practicing and adapting the material to fit your personality and situation, the routine should become natural. This word "natural" is very important. If your routines don't flow and aren't authentic, then you'll come across as a bad amateur stand-up comedian. It's better to use moderately funny original material than to fail using other people's material because you can't deliver their lines in a funny way. This is also why practice in low-pressure environments is important.

Also, you should always be creating and practicing new routines so you'll have a lot of material in your brain. If you see someone two days in a row, you don't want to repeat the same stuff or have nothing to say. Or if you have one routine, you don't want to go from the life of the party to a wallflower because your lack of material makes you look like a faker or a one hit wonder.

Your routines should also be adaptable to every situation. In many cases, it's just a matter of shifting a few details or mentally picking the right routine at the right time. This is important to remember because, as I mentioned in the last chapter, situational humor is more personal, which means you'll get the best laughs and be the most memorable. So, if you have a football routine about when you "wore your pants pads on the outside when you were ten and got laughed at" and you're with a bunch of quiz bowl members, then you could adapt it to the time you "totally froze during a class trivia game and got laughed at." Understand?

Also, routines should never be a crutch to avoid coming up with original material on the fly. Popular people are almost always popular because they have some original talent. Copy cats are never as beloved as the people they're copying. People love Justin Bieber (ok, some people), but no one, not even his biggest fans, cares about jbieberlover1998 singing one of his songs off key on YouTube.

If you are stuck and can't recall a topic for original routines, think about funny stories or memorable events from your life. Then adapt them to situations. Perhaps you can use a routine about getting lost when you went camping the time you were twelve. Or maybe you can focus on the time you accidentally got the car stuck in the mud when you parked in your yard. Just make sure your content is funny, authentic, and able to be adapted to any situation. Also, don't tell stories that make you look dumb or low-value. If it's a funny personal story, always make sure they are laughing with you, not at you.

To complete this chapter, write out at least two routines and practice them. I want these to be completely original. Make sure to throw in plenty of incongruity and observational humor, but don't violate the rule of safety. Include a short shaggy dog story or an example of anti-humor in one of them. The point here is to practice writing routines, not to write stand-up worthy material right now. If you want to write routines with a friend to bounce ideas off someone from the start, go ahead.

Next chance you get, I want you to practice what you've just written with someone you trust. These are your stories, so they should be natural and authentic. However, in high-stress environments like meeting strangers, you may not be able to deliver your routines with ease. So, have your friend or family member give you feedback, not only on the material itself, but also on your delivery, timing, and so on. Humor will probably be the most important weapon you have to influence and win over others. Don't take it lightly.

CHAPTER 15

THE WORLD IS YOUR HOOD

A guy I worked with several years ago was, in the teacher's lounge anyway, relaxed, cool, and fun to talk to. However, the word in the hallway was that he was a mean instructor. For whatever reason, this cool, laid-back guy, once he walked in the four walls of the classroom, became uptight, short-tempered, and acted like an educational dictator.

I can't tell you why my colleague acted this way. Perhaps he felt that being a successful educator required being dictatorial towards his students. Maybe the power that came from being "in charge" of a large number of teens went to his head. He may have even been terrified of managing a classroom of teens, and reacted by lashing out. Whatever his motives, this teacher illustrates an important point: not only do we act differently in different environments, but we can be successful in some and function poorly in others.

You've probably seen what I've described in action at your school. You may have a friend who is funny and outgoing during school, but at home, around his parents, seems shy and awkward. Or, maybe your girlfriend takes charge on the softball field, but clams up during science class. Our brains have learned that there are times we can be our true selves and other times we need to blend in. It's about survival. Perhaps your friend has mean parents and doesn't want to get in trouble. Maybe your girlfriend is lousy at science and doesn't want to get called on. Survival isn't just about preserving life, but also about not being humiliated or receiving an unflattering or unnecessary spotlight.

Think about the different environments you are in each day. If you're like the average teen, they're probably school, extracurricular activities, home, your social life, and maybe work. In each setting, you probably have sub-settings such as science class, debate team, etc. How would you describe yourself in each setting and sub-setting? Flexible or rigid? Detached or attached? In-charge or on the bottom of the pyramid? Do you exhibit your best qualities in each environment or only in a couple?

Most people will be closer to their best selves in one environment and farther in others. Typically, we act our best when we are either in-charge or confident about our abilities. It makes sense if you think about it. The unintelligent guy who does a great job catching a football will likely be confident and outgoing on the field, but may be awkward and quiet if he is participating in a quiz bowl match. In fact, when I talk to teens who aren't popular in general, I usually know they have fairly low self-esteem too. They can't be confident or in charge in any environment.

If you want to be really popular, you must be popular in every setting. Being liked by the geeks in your physics class is a start, but it's hardly popularity. If you can be liked by everyone in your science and gym classes, it's even better. But, your goal is to be popular and confident in the entire school (and beyond). There are a lot of people who really become popular everywhere they go. I know because I'm one of them. It's not that I walk into a room and instantly everyone sees me and says, "Wow, let's be his friend." No, I have the techniques to find them, win them over, and keep them as friends. You, through this book, are learning them too.

To be popular, you have to win people over in and out of the classroom.

Keep in mind that being popular is ultimately about making connections and winning fans. Obviously, recording a popular album or being in a hit movie is the fast way. But, if you become popular and liked in every environment, you'll be popular too. It's the slow way, but it works. Most people aren't going to be world-famous celebrities, but all people can be popular where they find themselves right now. That means you.

You're probably thinking a few things right now. Maybe you're excited, but nervous. Perhaps you're thinking of all the challenges at your school and that nauseated feeling is returning. Don't let the worry scare you. If you've been unpopular and lacking confidence your whole life, then breaking out of it will be a little scary. Being a shy wallflower is safe. However, if you truly want to be popular, and I believe you do, you'll have to take some leaps of faith. Just remember you'll have my advice as a guide.

For homework, I want you to refer back to your affirmations and declarations (Chapter 2) and the avatar you created based on them (Chapter 5). Write down every environment that you're in right now (school, home, etc.) and state how you can transform either yourself or the environment so that you're popular there. Then, write down concrete steps to achieve your goals. Remember that being popular everywhere you go typically involves becoming more relaxed and more confident or taking a leadership role. So, you should really be looking at two things.

The first is to think of ways you can rise to the top wherever you are. For example, if you are on the football team, but not starting, then you need to find ways to start. Maybe your concrete steps would be to lift weights more in the off season and practice an hour a day in the spring.

The second is to decide if you need to switch environments. Sometimes we're just simply a poor fit for the places we hang out. I knew a girl who was a genius at music, but went to a school where music wasn't really valued. They valued sports, which unfortunately for her popularity level, she didn't play. So, she wasn't terribly popular there. However, when she transferred to a school devoted entirely to music, she was one of everyone's favorite people. Her skills were valued and she was able to shine. While you may not be able to switch schools, maybe you can re-arrange classes, change activities, or take up new hobbies to create a fresh, "like new" environment.

When you've finished your list, do something to get the process of transformation started right now. I mean it. If your goal is to make the football team, then talk to your parents about joining a gym or starting a workout program tonight. If you need to join a new club, talk to the faculty adviser tomorrow. Just do it. Don't put it off.

And, remember that the more you become popular in every environment, the more you are expanding your friend base to become even more popular everywhere. Eventually, you want to be the person who's famous and beloved in whatever 'hood you're in. It may be hard to believe, but this is the lifestyle I (and other popular people) live.

CHAPTER 16

LOOKS AREN'T EVERYTHING (BUT THEY MATTER)

When I was in high school, I couldn't believe the taste some of the girls had in guys. I watched as boys, who quite frankly were ugly or very mediocre, dated some beautiful and popular ladies. I felt cheated because I, who worked out regularly and cared about my looks, was single while guys who obviously didn't care were more popular. I was indignant because in my mind "the system" had failed. I bought into the lie that in order to be popular, a person had to be good-looking.

You may be laughing as you read this, thinking my words are too good to be true. Maybe most of the popular people you know are good-looking. I'll agree that *most* younger celebrities and popular teenagers are good-looking. But, what matters is that not *all* of them are. That means that good looks aren't absolutely essential for being popular. But, as a result of the "looks are essential" myth, countless people who don't live up to Hollywood's impossible standards (photo-shopping anyone?) think they are doomed to be friendless and alone on weekends. Nothing could be further from the truth. You can be popular no matter how you look (within limits).

However, if you want to be popular, it never hurts to look your best. That's right. Less than stellar looks won't stop you from being popular, but studies and experience show that being pretty or handsome is an asset. Someone who is witty, charming, and talented will, in almost all cases, be popular. But, if he's witty, charming, talented, *and* handsome, then he will be even more popular.

Let's look at it this way. Your history teacher tells you that in order to pass his class, you need to get at least a seventy percent grade overall. However, he is generous and adds that taking notes every day will get you an automatic thirty percent added to your score. While you can't pass with *only* note taking, and you won't fail if you don't write down what he says, taking notes every class would certainly make your effort to pass easier because you'd only have forty percent to earn instead of the entire seventy.

Looks, in my opinion, work the same way as taking notes in this scenario. Good looks won't make you popular on their own. However, they certainly help and, if you've neglected your looks, you'd better change that attitude quickly.

When I say you should try to look good, don't get worried. I'm not talking about a Megan Fox or Robert Pattinson level of hotness.

Basically, I just want you to look your best at all times. That is what you see of almost every celebrity, even if they look their best according to their "image," which may be sloppy. It takes a lot of work for some of those guys to make their hair look like they just got out of bed.

Below are my general tips for looking your best. I'm not an expert by any means, but I do try to look good at all times, am healthy and fit, read up on the latest health and beauty news, and regularly receive fashion advice from professionals. If you have a huge need in the looks department (be honest with yourself here), consult an expert in that field (like a hair stylist, weight-loss consultant, etc.). But, these tips should at least help you make some minor adjustments and get you thinking about what it means to look your best.

Hygiene

Take regular showers and use deodorant. Bad smell is a huge turn-off for almost all people, whether when looking for friends or dating. Use cologne or perfume, but don't overdo it. You won't win friends if they're having an allergic reaction to you! Areas that can typically smell are orifices (that's all I'm going to say about this), the underarms, and the feet. Make sure all of these areas stay clean.

Another huge hygiene issue is bad breath. I knew a decent looking guy in high school who never had dates because of his horribly bad breath. Brush and floss each day, especially if you eat a lot of sugar or drink coffee or pop. Also, invest in an inexpensive "tongue-scraper." It isn't painful at all (despite how it sounds). Use it daily to break up the bacteria residing on your tongue. Believe it or not, most bad breath comes from the tongue and other fleshy areas around your teeth, so be sure to brush and scrape your entire mouth.

Clothes

Your clothes should be trendy, but not so trendy that you're just a clone. I personally don't believe in wearing shirts that advertise someone's brand. No offense to people who wear Hollister, Aeropostale, and Abercrombie and Fitch, but to me, those are so boring and common. Not only that, but you are paying for the privilege of advertising someone else's brand. Find your own unique (yet trendy) style and stick with it.

Also, be realistic with your clothes sizes. If you're pudgy, skip the skinny jeans and the tight tops. I went to summer camp once with a girl who obviously needed the next size jeans, but, for whatever reason, didn't make it to the clothing store. Also, if you're a guy, don't be too sloppy. Most guys are clueless about fashion. Even caring a little bit about your clothes (but not too much unless you're gay) will make you stand out with girls. As my fashion consultant friend told me: straight guys should be fashionable, but not too "fashion forward."

Make sure you wash your clothes too. You don't want to undo the benefits of a shower and deodorant because you've worn your favorite Nirvana shirt for three days in a row.

Hair and Face

Make sure your haircut is trendy. If you're a guy (and a girl!) avoid facial hair. Just because you can grow a bad high school mustache definitely doesn't mean you should. Also, wash your face and have enough facial hygiene to at least avoid excessive acne. Go to a doctor and get on medicine if your zits are horrible. Don't obsess with cleansing and washing, but do enough to avoid a greasy and gross looking face.

For girls, a trendy hairstyle is also a must since female styles tend to go out of fashion much more quickly than those of men. I went to school with a girl whose hair was so two years ago. And, she was mocked for it. It was wrong and stupid to make fun of her, but it happened. Be aware of it.

Also, really short hair may be easier, but it is never preferable. If you want to look attractive to guys, keep it at least shoulder length. As for your makeup, be trendy as well. And if you cake on the makeup because you have something to hide, everyone else knows what you're doing. So, just be natural. If you don't believe me, go to epicfail.com and see all the jokes made about girls who put on too much makeup.

Oh, and duck faces belong on ducks, not humans. Be natural when you smile.

Hands and Feet

You may not think much about either of these body parts,

especially if you're a man. However, people who are more observant care about the look of your hands and feet. So, at least give them a second thought.

Make sure your hands are clean and well-groomed. Don't bite your nails and make sure to clean dirt out of them. Also, it never hurts to moisturize your hands. Dry, cracked hands, which are common in winter, are gross. No girl or guy will want to hold those hands. A minute of applying lotion a couple times a day should help stop the cracking.

For your feet, it's important to keep them clean. Change socks at least daily (sometimes more if you're sweaty). If your feet smell particularly bad, then you may want to use some kind of odor eater in your shoe. Speaking of shoes, don't let them get all gross and smelly. Wash them occasionally. Trust me; "feet smell" is very nasty and unattractive.

Height

For women, this advice is also second nature. If you're really short you can wear heels; if you're really tall and don't want to appear too manly, wear flats. No biggie.

For men, the issue is different. Society tends to value tallness, but short of the platform shoe craze of the 70s, hasn't really provided short males with a socially acceptable way to increase their stature. If you're short, you have a couple options. The first is to do nothing. You don't have to be tall to be popular, even with women. However, I don't recommend wearing clothes that accentuate your shortness. You'll want to avoid horizontal stripes, baggy clothes, big patterns (for example, larger squares on sweaters), and weird color schemes. These all make you look shorter. Instead wear close-fitting clothing, single color schemes, and smaller patterns.

You could also enhance your height in some fashion. You can do this by purchasing shoes with larger heels or even shoes with lifts. Insertable lifts are available too. If you increase your height by a couple of inches, make sure you can still walk. And avoid situations where you may be asked to remove your shoes. Society already thinks short people are insecure and the last thing you want to do is confirm that impression. Not only that, but you don't want to lose four inches in gym class when you switch to tennis shoes.

Weight

Being fat won't stop you from being popular. We all know overweight people who are popular. Actor and musician Jack Black is one example. However, the truth is most people will find you more attractive in the broad sense of the word if you are skinny, but not too skinny. Research seems to indicate that the "fit" look is most attractive. However, this does not mean extreme muscle gain, for either guys or girls. Losing weight and getting generally in shape have other advantages as well. You can fit into trendier clothing, won't sweat as much, and probably have fewer health problems.

One of the trends I noticed as a teacher is that my students were getting chubbier each year. Research confirms my observation: children and teens are becoming more overweight. However, Hollywood continually tells us that the "super thin" look is in, for both guys and girls. It's really tough when people are getting bigger, but the supposed ideal is getting smaller. Ultimately, you can't be concerned with the Hollywood image. Eat right and get in shape, and you will be fine.

Your homework is to write down areas where you think you need to improve your looks. For each area you write down, come up with a few ways you can make yourself look better. They can be little things you can do now or possibly long-term solutions that involve a professional. Maybe creating a checklist is in order for certain hygiene issues (e.g. brush twice a day, remember deodorant, etc.).

Remember that before starting any health improvement program, you should consult your doctor and parents, to make sure you are making genuinely healthy lifestyle changes.

CHAPTER 17

SHOW YOUR WORTH

Let me lay out a scenario for you. I'm sitting in a busy coffee shop and watch several customers come in. One is about seventeen years old. He walks up to the register with confidence. While there, he jokes around with the girl taking his order. He's wearing a varsity jacket that tells the world he's involved in baseball, basketball, and choir. The girl messes up his order, but he laughs it off. As he's leaving the restaurant, he holds the door for another customer and starts chatting with that guy. The young lady at the register asks her friend, "Do you think that guy's single?"

Another guy comes in, also about seventeen years old. He's overweight and doesn't smell the best. He has sweat stains under his armpits. He timidly approaches the register and mumbles his order. The girl has to ask him to repeat himself and he gets impatient with her. When she tells him he has to wait for his bagel because they're just finishing up the baking, he snaps at her again. He leaves with his head down and wearing a frown. The girl at the register tells her friend, "Sheesh, what a creeper."

Which of the two guys do you think appeared "high-value" that day? In other words, who appeared as a person who would be "worth" knowing? Who appeared "low-value," meaning not "worth" knowing? Although everyone has different tastes, most people of all ages, male and female, would rather be friends with or date a relaxed, talented, and funny guy instead of a sweaty, impatient, and frowning jerk.

One of the biggest keys to being popular is to project your high-value to the world. Everyone who becomes popular offers something of value to other people. They have worth for their power, money, ability to entertain, sporting talent, intelligence, and even looks. Yes, some people have value because others like to stare at them. Whatever the reason, a popular person of any age is worth knowing. Unpopular people are generally not worth knowing because they typically offer little in the way of value to the world. Either that, or they are poor at communicating their worth to others.

Look around at the popular people in your school. Chances are they have a talent of some kind. It could be sports, acting, singing, or playing an instrument. Maybe they're very fashion forward, are really funny, or are just easy on the eyes. Whatever their particular talent, they are popular because large numbers of people value them. They have something inside of them or an incredible talent that makes them worth befriending.

Give me ten minutes with any high school yearbook and I can tell you more or less who the most popular kids are. They're the ones who are involved in activities. If I see a guy who's on the basketball and baseball teams, involved in the Fellowship of Christian Athletes, a member of Honor Society, and a participant in Student Council, I can be pretty certain this guy is popular.

On the other hand, if I see a girl who played volleyball as a freshman and was in the Garden club as a junior, but nothing else, I can probably conclude (unless she's super beautiful) she's not very popular. It's because when you get involved, have hobbies, and nurture talents, you're increasing the value you offer to others.

Right now, you may doubt your value. You may not be good-looking and you may not be involved in any school activities. On your bad days, you may not treat people very well. Are you low-value or high-value? Maybe you're somewhere in between, which can happen sometimes. Give an honest answer. Also, make sure that what you have to offer is something the world considers valuable. When I was in fifth grade, I was really upset that I beat a tough boss in *Super Mario Brothers 2* and no one cared.

If you think you're high-value, then your goal is simply to project it more often. I've devoted a whole chapter to this called "Promote Yourself First" (Chapter 21). That will give you advice on how to promote yourself in a way that doesn't come across as arrogant. If you've determined you're low-value, then you have to raise your value.

The first and best way for a teenager to raise his or her value is to find a talent and actively showcase that. Normally, this means getting involved in some sport, organization, or activity (or taking lessons of some kind). This has the added benefit of introducing you to new people, many of whom will like you or admire you for your talent which you share with them.

For example, my freshman year, we were herded into the gymnasium to watch our yearly high school talent contest. I remember laughing when I saw a group of boys on the lineup, thinking that the students listed on the bill didn't really have a whole lot of talent. I found out when they got on stage that they were a band and I think I yawned. Then, they played an amazing version of "Enter Sandman" by the heavy metal band Metallica. At the end of the song, the entire student body was on its feet! Let's just say they were all pretty popular after that.

In the age of the internet and YouTube, even the dumbest, most ridiculous "talent" can launch someone into popularity. I can't stand "Fred Figglehorn" and his humor. But, what I think doesn't matter. The guy behind "Fred," Lucas Cruikshank, is popular and I'm guessing wealthy too. It may be bad news for some people, but your talent, no matter how crazy or silly, could be enough to make you very popular. And, that is good news – for you anyway.

Even as a teacher, I found that talent was an important part of the respect and popularity I had with my students. They liked me because I wasn't just a teacher, but a funny person, athlete, writer, etc. Although my teaching abilities were important, whether or not they liked me (popularity) depended a lot on whether or not I was good at a lot of the things they thought mattered.

I hope you can see where I'm going with this. People who are very involved in high school activities or nurture talents outside of school do so because they have something to offer the school, their fellow students, and even the world-at-large. As a result, their classmates typically like them. For example, a baseball team that wins a conference championship offers the teachers, students, and alumni a feeling of pride and accomplishment as a community.

If you're not talented at anything and don't have the time or inclination to become a guitar hero or a star running-back, don't worry. My second tip to become high-value is a little easier. It's humor. Truly funny people are pretty rare in this world, which is why good comedians are well-compensated. If something is rare, then people assign it more value. Be funny and share it with others and they will consider you valuable (see Chapter 13).

Another fairly easy way to show high-value is to be outgoing. How many new people talk to you on a daily basis? One? Two? Sometimes I'll wager you may go a whole week and not have anyone new approach you and talk to you. Striking up a conversation with new people and getting to know them better shows that you are a confident and high-value person because so few people approach strangers on a regular basis.

Taking charge of situations and groups also shows you are high-value. While some teens have started their own non-profits or businesses, most likely you're not in charge of much, whether it's home, school, or work.

Many teens own businesses, which shows excellence, and gives them extra money.

However, I'd recommend you try to be in charge of something, anything. Start a group at school, coordinate volunteers for a charity event or run for president of an existing school organization. Create an underground newspaper. Teach Sunday school. Organize a park cleanup. Do anything that puts you in charge of others. It's an added bonus if what you do interests a lot of people because then you can be in charge of large numbers and use them to meet even more people. Just remember to be cool and relaxed and not let the power go to your head.

Another tip to be high-value is to simply avoid doing things perceived as low-value. That's right, sometimes by not making too many mistakes, you can fake it. Some examples of low-value behavior are (which are common among teens): arrogance, whining, playing the victim, timidity, being uptight, rigid and/or controlling, outbursts of anger, lacking composure in stressful situations, being a tattle-tale, etc. Avoid these and anything else you think will make you look less valuable in the eyes of others, and you've already won half the battle.

The best way to act with high-value on a daily basis is to ask yourself a simple question: "If I saw someone else acting this way, would I consider him or her worth knowing?" If your tastes are unusual, then replace "I" with "the average person." In most cases, you should be able to figure it out. For example, walking with your head down and mumbling isn't valuable in anyone's book. On the other hand, organizing a canned food drive for your church or school would be almost universally admired.

Right now, I'd like you to list ways in which you are talented and high-value. If you're not high-value enough, which is probably the case since we can all become more valuable, then write down traits you can work on and actions you can take to become more worth knowing. Remember my tips and focus especially on how you can become more involved in school activities and better show off your talents. Check your list from Chapter 15 if you're having trouble coming up with good ideas.

Finally, I'd like you to really focus on getting into the excellent mindset, both now and for the rest of your life. Commit to be a genuinely excellent and outstanding person in all that you do. If you want, add "achieving excellence" and "being the best at all you do" to your affirmations and declarations. Remember, being a popular teenager isn't your only goal. You want to be popular and successful throughout your entire life.

CHAPTER 18

POPULARITY'S GOLDEN RULE: BE COOL

One of my favorite hangouts is a coffee shop called Tim Hortons. I not only like the coffee, but find the atmosphere conducive to writing and spending time with family and friends. I travel frequently around Ohio and always make it a point to stop at the various Tim Hortons locations along the way, as well as interact and build relationships with the regular employees.

One day, as I was visiting one of my favorite locations, I noticed they were having a corporate visit. In addition to the people in suits walking around with clipboards, one of the biggest clues was how stressed everyone looked. I was my usual charming self, but I also realized how that day, the employees, three of whom had become friends, needed more than just a little humor and conversation. They also needed me to make them look good in front of the regional manager. So, I approached him, introduced myself, and told him what a great Tim Hortons location that was. I also told him how the employees were a huge part of my positive experience.

Be cool…but not cold.

Afterward, a group of employees approached me and thanked me. One of them, speaking for their co-workers, said, "That was really cool." In fact, that word – cool – has been thrown around a lot about me (and my friends and business associates), from the way I treat hired help to my reputation as a fun and popular teacher. Almost all young people use that word a lot, but do they really even know its meaning? Although we usually know cool when we see it, a cool person is someone who is relaxed, fun, funny, a little edgy, somewhat mysterious, and, above all, a person we'd like to befriend and even date.

What that definition means, of course, is that if you want to be popular, then you must become "cool," especially if you are a guy. I'm going to address a few ways that you can be cool, although keep in mind the general principles of this book are ultimately designed to create cool people. This chapter simply summarizes some particular aspects of becoming cool in one spot.

First, "cool" is ultimately a mindset. Remember Chapter 2 and the discussion about perspective? Well, being cool means adopting a cool perspective. This means that you don't merely do cool things, but that your mindset, or indeed your very being, becomes cool. In other words, being cool becomes second nature to you. You always approach a situation as a flexible (see Chapter 9), detached (see Chapter 12), and fun person. People know that whenever they need an energy boost, a laugh, or a chance for fun and excitement, they can count on you.

Second, being cool involves being easygoing. The word cool ultimately derives from being calm, usually in the face of some stress. This is a highly valued trait, and all good leaders possess coolness in the face of great danger. The soldier who can stay calm and focused in battle will be a better leader to his troops than someone who has a nervous breakdown or runs for the hills. The same is true of you in the "battle zone" of the modern high school.

If you are a hothead, drama queen, or hopelessly insecure, then you'll never truly be cool. You'll have to learn to relax and be more detached. If someone gets you angry, you don't erupt. If you hear a rumor, you refuse to pass it along or dwell on it. If someone makes fun of your glasses, you laugh it off. And, so forth. You have to chill out in most stressful situations and not succumb to the typical drama of high school (see Chapter 19).

However, don't confuse being cool and easygoing with being passive. You never want to be passive. You should assert yourself (but never be aggressive) when necessary. Keep in mind that people who are cool in the face of extreme stress (like soldiers or world leaders) are relaxed, but that relaxation allows them the presence of mind to act decisively and assertively when needed. So, be laid-back about the unimportant things, but assert yourself when it's important.

For example, if you are being bullied, you should stand up for yourself. The same is true if you want to share your opinion or express yourself. However, if someone takes the last of the mini-pizzas in the cafeteria line before you, don't throw a tantrum; just get something else. I've devoted a whole section later in the book on how to properly assert yourself (see Chapter 27).

Third, have a bit of an edge. You don't want to be an unattractive jerk (see next paragraph), but you also can't be bland and totally predictable. Being cool also means providing people with some degree of fun and excitement. You can be fun and exciting, but in a way that doesn't put you or others in danger or gets you punished by your parents, the school, or the police. I address this edginess in more detail later (see Chapter 33). Make sure to read that chapter before attempting anything remotely adventurous.

Finally, being cool is largely about not being unattractive. Yes, like with being high-value, you can fake being cool by avoiding certain bad behaviors. There are many traits that make a person unattractive, and I'll give you a few: tattling on others, gossiping, whining, causing trouble, being too needy, and instigating problems between friends. So, to be cool, cultivate values that are the exact opposite of these traits: being loyal, keeping secrets, showing gratitude, helping others, asserting independence, and bringing people together. You can think of more, I'm sure.

Being a genuinely cool person (maybe you already are) will go a long way towards making you popular. I was talking to my friends just the other day about how awesome it is to encounter truly cool people, the ones who are relaxed and don't give others grief all the time. Think about how truly rare it is to find genuinely cool people, whether among your friends, classmates, or the adults you know. If you become a cool person, people of all ages will want to be around you. Actually, not just want to be around you, but flock to your side.

I was reading a story a couple of years ago about a woman who researched her high school classmates later in life to see who had been the most successful after graduation. It wasn't the football captain, head cheerleader, or valedictorian. Nope. It was a cool guy who stayed out of the drama and was liked by pretty much everyone in the school.

He had landed a high profile position as the Vice President of a very successful company. And he did it because he related well to people and treated them with respect, a pattern that he first developed in high school. So, the choices and changes you are making now are setting you up for greater success later in life too. The workplace needs cool people too, believe me.

For homework, I'd like you to write a list of people that you think are cool. Beside their name, write out a few traits that make them cool in your mind. Maybe you'd pick your guitar-playing neighbor because he belts out a great version of your favorite song. Maybe it's your coach because he was there for you during a rough time and wins games. Remember that everyone has faults, so keep the focus on why this person is cool.

After compiling this list, come up with your top five "cool" traits. Write a few steps that you can take to start living these traits. Or, if you already have some of them, list how you can develop even more confidence and greater mastery of them in the future.

CHAPTER 19

SAVE THE DRAMA (AND NOT EVEN FOR YOUR MAMA)

One August morning, I walked into a "civil war" in the office where I had a summer job. It turns out that one employee hadn't invited another employee to a party. The uninvited individual was offended (and hurt), and everyone in the office, except for me and one other person, took a side. The entire department was almost split down the middle in supporting either the party's host or the uninvited guest. Even my friend and I who refused to "get involved" were still involved as we had to listen to the daily drama. When we refused to take sides, the entire office became mad at us!

I tell this story for a couple of reasons. The first is to illustrate that adults are just as capable of drama as teenagers. The second is to show just how dumb and petty most drama turns out to be when you look back on it. Oh, and there is a third reason: drama is destructive, very destructive, both to individuals and to institutions.

This one little party and lack of an invitation wreaked havoc on an entire organization. While the social aspects of the company became tense (like separate tables at lunch and awkward moments at the coffeemaker) and personal friendships broke down, the fundamental purpose of the company suffered most. One department suddenly became, in practice, two, and doing any activity smoothly (like helping customers) became much more difficult. Only when the boss stepped in did the nonsense stop. Both sides valued their job security more than their feuding and stopped the drama. But, by that point lots of damage had already been done.

If you are a high school student, especially a female one, I'm sure you have more than enough experience with drama. I don't want to sound sexist, but if you looked at the characters in the above drama, the entire office staff involved in the fighting was female. The only ones who stayed out of it were men. Men can get involved in drama just as easily as anyone else, of course. Yet, this chapter will be particularly important for my female readers since drama, at any age, seems to be a bigger problem with the ladies (don't be offended since we guys have our share of unique problems too).

Right now, you're probably running some of your own dramatic experiences through your head. I was caught up in more than my fair share of conflict as a teenager, even if I didn't start it. I can remember the gossip, rumors, prank phone calls (the availability of caller ID eventually put a stop to that), and all sorts of other things my friends and I wasted our time on. While you probably know that drama can be painful, I hope you also realize it's ultimately pointless. Yes, that is the number one reason to avoid drama: it's completely a waste of your time, which should be used to become more popular and happy.

When I taught high school, I couldn't believe the crazy things students fought over. Some of the issues, like boyfriends or girlfriends, I can understand (at least somewhat). But, other times, I couldn't see any reason for the drama. Both sides would tell me separately they hated it, but yet neither side would stop. In some cases, the fighting quite literally took over the lives of these teenagers so that their days were spent furthering the rivalry at school, while the evenings were wasted continuing it on social networking. Oh, and sometimes they had trouble sleeping over the stress. What a literal waste of precious time (see Chapter 32).

I'm not going to give you any surefire tips for ending drama. If you develop those tips yourself, then contact me immediately, so I can pass along that information to the United Nations and the heads of the world's nations. Fighting and conflict have always been part of our world, from individual friendships to international borders, and sadly, will likely never end. However, I am going to share basic advice to handle drama, so that you don't start it and don't get sucked in.

The first tip to deal with drama is to not sweat the small stuff. The best piece of advice I received as a teacher came from an old teaching manual written in the 1800s. It said that sometimes when a teacher sees a student misbehaving the teacher should actually...gasp...ignore it!

The reasoning was that sometimes, especially on little matters, it simply wasn't worth the ensuing headache to deal with an unimportant discipline issue.

The words of wisdom from the teacher's manual should be your goal too. Sometimes it's just best to ignore the nonsense you encounter in school, especially the little things. Don't spread the gossip, no matter how juicy. Avoid starting or embellishing rumors, even if you don't like the person who is the subject of the rumor. If someone is trying to get you riled up or aggravated, walk away. While there are times you'll need to assert yourself (see Chapter 27), if it's a small matter and likely to fuel drama, then ignore it.

Second, find something better to do. This is similar to the advice of ignoring, but solves the issue that leads to most drama: boredom. One of my students was involved in two sports leagues and got straight A's. I don't recall her ever starting or engaging in drama. I don't know if she even had the time. If you have the time to forward gossipy text messages, or get your friends fighting each other, then you need to get a life. Join a sports team or find a good club. If you're so great at drama, maybe take up acting. Successful people are typically too busy being successful to have time for drama.

Finally, step away from the situation. A lot of drama comes, quite simply, from misunderstandings. Although we may want to deny it, most people starting and continuing drama aren't inherently bad. For whatever reason, they seriously believe they've been wronged. Think about the times you stirred up trouble. Likely you didn't say, "I'm going to be a jerk this morning" when you got out of bed. Nope. You probably felt genuinely bothered by what someone else did and drama was the only way you knew to deal with it.

Next time you are annoyed or experience stress, take a step back from it and look at it objectively, like you're not involved in it. This is detachment (see Chapter 12) because you are un-attaching yourself from a situation. You are removing yourself emotionally from the equation and looking at it rationally. Ask yourself questions like:

- Why did the person act the way he or she did?

- Could I be thinking the worst of the other person while giving myself the benefit of the doubt (this happens a lot in disputes)?

- What would be a positive response to this person or situation that would make it better, rather than make it worse?

- What response would ultimately make me more liked and popular?

The last question is my favorite. Creating drama divides people and destroys friendships. Being popular is a numbers game that involves bringing people together (towards you) and creating friendships. Which choice will you make?

I want to say one word about your family before I end the chapter. While families aren't perfect, in the vast majority of cases, your parents and siblings (and other family members) love you and want the best for you. They've also invested more time, money, and emotional capital in you than you'll probably ever realize (until you become a parent, that is). So, give them a break on the drama too. Step back from your fights with them and ask the same questions I listed previously. Just because they have to love you doesn't mean they should have to put up with your crap.

Your homework for this chapter is to take some past dramatic situations and list them. It could be any type of serious friction, whether it's with friends, family, acquaintances, etc. For each one, list the negative choices you made in that drama. For example, maybe you made up a rumor about a popular girl who didn't invite you to her birthday party, or you bullied a kid who was weird. Then, I want you to list ways you could've resolved the situation positively. For example, you could say how you should've talked to the popular girl and told her how she hurt your feelings, or you could try to be more inclusive and understanding of the odd kid.

Now, go out and try to resolve your current and future dramas in a positive and popularity-affirming way. And, remember, save your drama. Not for your mama; just save it, period.

CHAPTER 20

BREAK FROM THE HERD

One season the American version of the show *X-Factor* featured Drew Ryniewicz, a young contestant who began her performance by sharing her love for Justin Bieber (she was going to sing one of his songs). As a non-fan of both Justin Bieber and copycats, I'll admit, I groaned. I figured she'd get up there, give a bland, typical performance of a Bieber song and be tossed off the stage.

Wrong! She grabbed the microphone, kept cool in the face of the judges trying to make her nervous, and performed a very original and bold version of "Baby." Even Simon Cowell was impressed, not just by her amazing voice, but because a fourteen year old could be so original and daring with an established song.

Most of us aren't like Drew. Instead of venturing out and trying something new, we prefer the safety of the familiar, whether songs or anything else. It's actually pretty understandable. Humans are weak and puny compared to saber-toothed tigers and wooly mammoths. We banded together into herds (which we call communities or tribes) because of the safety that came with numbers. By working together, early humans cooperated to achieve more than they ever could have accomplished as individuals. This intelligent cooperation has led to civilization as we know it.

Being away from the herd means you are in control.

However, while the herd is safe, it isn't always the best place if you want to be noticed. Look at a bunch of zebras running on the African plains. Can you tell one from another? Probably not. But humans are nothing like that, right? Well, how about the number of white shirts and ties on the subway any weekday morning? If you still aren't convinced, count the number of Hollister, Aeropostale, or Abercrombie and Fitch shirts you see when you walk down a typical public school hallway. So many of us just love to blend in.

If you want to be popular, you must separate from the herd. In the 21st century, this simply means you must be original and create your own path. However, doing your own thing can still be scary because you'll leave the safety of the group. You may not have to dodge lions and tigers, but you may still be made fun of, ridiculed, and even bullied. But, if you're successful, the reward can be great.

In the early 1950s music had become boring and stale. "How Much Is That Doggie In the Window?" was a number one hit for *eight weeks* in 1953. This lame trend in music led several musicians to rebel from the mainstream, to break away and do their own thing (8). The result was rock-and-roll as we know it. In the beginning, rock music was denounced as evil, anti-Christian, and a corrupter of youth. That's right. Acts like Buddy Holly and Elvis Presley, which your grandparents listened to, were "of the devil!"

It seems silly now, but records were smashed, songs were banned, and pastors condemned the new music from church pulpits. However, the musical artists who started rock-and-roll broke from the herd and, like a purple zebra, exposed themselves to the (metaphorical) lions. They blazed a new trail and found countless followers. There was a herd, but they formed it and were at the front of it. They were popular in their day and now are considered innovators and musical legends.

Your challenge is to stand out in your own way. After all, most teens will likely encounter hundreds of people every day, especially during the school year. In the majority of cases, everyone they meet is almost exactly the same in personality, style, and blandness. If someone meets you, what makes you worthy of their attention? If you're not unique in some way, you may tag along with the popular kids, but you likely won't be truly popular yourself. The reason is simple: you're forgettable! Just like everyone else.

You're probably thinking I'm going to tell you to break from the herd by "being yourself." Well, I'm not. "Just be yourself" is horrible advice. For one, most people don't like themselves and this is in spite of being told to "be yourself" from at least the time they entered school. My advice is to always *be your best self*. Take the traits you wrote down in your goals (Chapter 2) and gave to your avatar (Chapter 5) and actually live them. Hopefully you put some big dreams in there. Go out and live them and you will have no trouble breaking from the herd.

Although I address this issue in more depth later (See Chapter 24), I hope it goes without saying that being a freak isn't the same as breaking from herd. Yes, being weird will probably get you out of the herd (kicked out!), but you won't get any followers. A serial killer is unique, but other than fellow twisted human beings, he's not going to have a lot of friends and genuine admirers.

Your homework is to list ten things that are unique about you.

These are your interests, talents, style, etc. that separate you from the herd. Think about how the average person looks, acts, etc. and how you deviate from them (in a positive way, of course). Maybe you are happy first period when everyone else is grumpy from waking up early. Maybe you have a photographic memory. Whatever you identify as your unique traits, write them down.

If you can't think of any unique traits, then you need to go re-read Chapter 17 and double your efforts at becoming more talented and high-value. If you can become multi-talented and worthy of being known, then you should have no trouble finding things to write down.

Next, I want you to think about ways your unique self can shine through everywhere. Think about how you act at school, at work, or in social settings. Chances are you conform for the sake of emotional safety.

I'd like you to try to break out of that routine a little bit. Don't do anything that will get you arrested, suspended, or sent to the mental ward, but try to make your unique traits evident in environments where you normally act like everyone else. An example would be where I talked about the band that played Metallica in front of the school. No one even knew they were talented. When everyone found out, they were invited to a lot more parties.

Being your best self may be scary at first. It's natural to feel this way. However, remember that you want to be successful and popular, not just an ordinary person. You want to be extraordinary and have the benefits that come from that (like fun, lots of dates, amazing friendships, etc.).

Gradually, you'll find it easier to let the best traits of your true self shine before everyone. I think you'll discover that people around you will begin to appreciate your independence and uniqueness. However, if you find that your true self isn't welcome in certain places or with certain friends, then it's probably time to find places and friends where your best self is more accepted. Remember, you create your own reality. Others don't create it for you.

CHAPTER 21

PROMOTE YOURSELF FIRST

A few months ago I read an article about a guy from Ohio who was a huge Boston Celtics fan. This guy was known around his town for having Celtics memorabilia filling his entire house, which he'd proudly show to anyone who visited. He even drove a Celtics themed truck.

Oh, and he once *almost* met Larry Bird, Boston's legendary forward. Now, I'm sure he's a good guy and he must be fairly successful to afford all this Celtics stuff. But, come on! Here's a guy who spends much of his free time promoting someone else and he only got to "almost" meet Larry Bird.

Before you judge too harshly, go to your closet or dresser right now. How many Abercrombie, Hollister, Aeropostale, or Old Navy shirts do you have, almost all of which have the brand displayed prominently? What about the college or professional team's shirts you wear around all the time? Or the teen idol you have hanging on your wall whose birthday, eye color, and other vital stats you can recite by heart? Suddenly, the Boston Celtics guy isn't so weird, huh?

I don't want to imply that there's anything necessarily wrong with wearing clothes that advertise a brand, or having a healthy admiration for sports stars. I'll admit without hesitation that every Sunday in the fall and winter I want to be in front of a television watching the Cleveland Browns lose. I also buy every Killers album the day it comes out.

However, I'm amazed by the number of people, both teens and adults, who live bland, boring lives they hate, but rather than coming up with ways to be popular and successful and promote themselves, they devote their energy to making other people and organizations more popular.

I was raised to be humble, which I still believe can be virtuous. However, you're only humble if you have a skill or trait to be humble about. Most of us don't talk about ourselves, but it's not because we've mastered humility. Rather, we don't promote ourselves out of fear, lack of confidence in our abilities, or low self-esteem. This is not being humble, but being afraid.

I also believed a terrible myth that true talent and ability would always be recognized and no one should ever promote themselves. Let me tell you from personal experience: that advice is crappy. Promote yourself and do it before you promote anyone else. If you have a talent, express it to anyone who's interested and even those who may not be at first. The worst anyone can say is "no" and if you hear "yes" then the sky could be the limit.

I know a teenager who wants to be a musician, but her time is rarely spent singing or even learning an instrument. She admits she hates to read and learn new things. She won't sing in public for fear of rejection. I guess she must think that some random stranger will see her, guess that she likes singing (she won't sing in public, remember?), and sign her to a multimillion dollar recording contract. Sorry, but it doesn't happen that way.

I know another guy who, as a sophomore in high school, started working on a screenplay. He put a lot of time and effort into it, proudly told others about it, and always remained open to feedback. In addition, he's naturally smart and pays attention to the world around him.

While no one pursuing a dream has a sure road to success, which of the two previous examples is likely to have the greatest chance of succeeding? I think you know the answer. A person who works hard, learns from his or her mistakes, and pursues the dream will have a much better chance of achieving that dream than someone who sits around fantasizing about a goal. Yep, if you want to succeed, you have to know the difference between a dream and a fantasy.

You may be thinking it's arrogant to always be tooting your own horn. It can be. However, there's a difference between bragging and demonstrating your talents. If you constantly talk about how awesome you are at baseball, but can't even throw one, that's arrogance. If, however, you promote yourself to a coach and go out and throw a 90 mph fastball, then you're just being truthful. If you have an awesome talent, great idea, or something else that is unique and valuable, then you have to share it and get it out in the world yourself.

Keep in mind too that a genuinely talented individual meets the needs of other people. Someone who is a good listener meets the need of another human being who has problems that need shared. A talented athlete meets the need of a coach and organization that value the talent. A great guitarist meets the need of a group of people who love guitar music. I could go on and on, but I hope you get the point: your talent isn't just about you, but also about helping and/or entertaining others.

I talk about my business all the time (I basically offer popularity advice in various settings) and people love it. In fact, in almost every case, they like it so much they want to be a part of it in some way. So, by promoting myself, everyone wins. I get new contacts for my business, and the people I meet either benefit from what I offer, or get to share in my success ("give-get-give" remember?).

In order to self-promote, you must keep a few things in mind. First, don't lie about yourself and your talents. If you suck at cheerleading, don't tell everyone you're the best cheerleader in your county. However, you must always put the best spin on what you do.

Think of a real estate agent trying to sell a tiny house. A good realtor knows it's not small; it's cozy.

Also, you don't have to dwell on your failures or focus on your shortcomings. In fact, avoid talking about them unless you're in a position where full disclosure is absolutely required. For example, if you've put on twenty pounds of muscle and can run a forty in 4.5 seconds, there's no need to mention the time you were cut from the pee-wee football team when you were seven.

Second, if you have a talent, awesome trait, or great idea, be passionate and positive about it. There's nothing wrong with being excited about yourself. Confidence is a highly valued trait. And, make sure you're also passionate about sharing your accomplishments with others. If you don't have enthusiasm for what you do, then your talents or ideas aren't going to reach very many people or make you very popular.

My third tip is to always be adequately prepared to promote yourself. I know it sounds weird for a teenager, but you should always have something you can give people who are interested in knowing you better. Maybe even get a cool business card with your name, phone number, twitter username, etc. on it (be sure to read Chapter 37 before you do this).

Also, take advantage of every social media opportunity to connect with others. You never know when writing on someone's Facebook wall, making a random tweet, or following up with someone popular could lead to you becoming more popular and successful. Do the research on your area of talent, connect with others who share your passion and learn from them, and pretty much do anything necessary to get your talent out to as many people as possible. Remember, popularity is ultimately a numbers game.

Finally, don't be afraid to be a little edgy. Take the example of Brian Bosworth, a first round draft pick by the Seattle Seahawks of the National Football League in 1987. His football career was cut short due to injuries, but he was an expert at getting attention. He once flew into football practice in a helicopter. Was it a little arrogant and probably annoying to some of the older players? Yes. Did the national media jump all over it and make him a household name? Yes!

Later when the Seahawks played the Denver Broncos, Bosworth mouthed off about John Elway, Denver's now legendary quarterback. Broncos fans were so outraged that ten thousand of them bought fifteen-dollar "Ban the Boz" T-shirts and wore them to the Seahawks game. It turns out Bosworth's company produced the shirts and he made a ton of money in the process (9).

You could benefit from well-planned and appropriate stunts. However, keep in mind that you are becoming popular while keeping your values. You don't want to do anything that gets you in trouble with your parents, the school, or the law. You also must avoid anything that mocks others or makes them feel bad about themselves. You want to win fans, not alienate them. Keep it moral, legal, ethical, and appropriate.

Also don't be creepy. I knew a guy in junior high who had a bunch of flowers delivered in science class to a girl he had a crush on, but had never talked to previously. Sure, it was outrageous and a risk, but it backfired and she was so creeped out she asked to be transferred out of his class. Being outrageous doesn't have to be immoral, criminal, or creepy.

Some examples of possible stunts would be coming to school in a Hawaiian shirt and shorts during winter, showing up to the football game in a giant chicken costume, etc. At the school where I taught, an uptight, nerd type of guy wore a very funny outfit to the Halloween dress up day. Everyone was shocked that he would do that and I heard all day from students how cool he was. It's a great example of a risk that worked.

If you can pull off a stunt like that, then try it. Make it small, if necessary, like wearing a weird outfit or breaking out of your comfort zone. If you don't think you can successfully do it, then it's best to avoid it. You don't want to look stupid in front of large numbers of people if you're not ready. See Chapter 33 for more about appropriate risk-taking.

So, get out there and start promoting yourself first. For homework, I'd like to you to put a plan of action together to promote yourself. For the previous chapter, you should've listed some of your unique traits. Pick a couple of them and come up with action steps to get your talents noticed. Be specific. If you are funny, then write down, "Get a YouTube account, borrow flip camera from Johnny, etc."

By promoting yourself and your talents, you'll meet new people and win new fans, both very important to becoming popular. In addition, by nurturing your talents and bettering yourself as a teenager, you're setting yourself up for greater financial and social success later in life.

CHAPTER 22

YOU GOTTA ASK

For my twelfth birthday, I wanted a Walkman, a portable cassette player, more than just about anything. I could practically hear U2's music being pumped right into my ears as I walked down the streets of my small town listening to my cassette tapes, and showing everyone how awesome I was. Don't laugh; someday you will tell stories about obsolete technology.

After unwrapping all of the presents at my birthday party, mom and dad brought out a "surprise" package that was just "Walkman" sized (they were huge compared to modern iPods). I opened it with eager anticipation.

Five minutes later, I abruptly left my party to pout in my bedroom, acting like a spoiled brat with my Walkman, my *radio* Walkman, sitting on the bed. When mom and dad came upstairs and I explained my extreme disappointment, they calmly and politely pointed out that I had never actually asked for a Walkman that played cassettes. Oops.

While I can look back on my stupidity with a sense of humor, most people still don't realize a truth so great that even Jesus taught it: ask and you shall receive. While Jesus was talking about asking God in prayer, what he says applies to many other situations as well. All too often, we never end up getting what we want because we're too afraid to ask for it.

This chapter is closely related to the previous chapter's advice on self-promotion. I mentioned how if you don't promote yourself then no one else is going to either. The same principle is true for getting what you want, whether it's a chance for an extra credit assignment in math class, or an opportunity to audition in front of a famous record producer.

You'll never get any opportunities unless you take the initiative and ask for them. Most people in positions of power are far too busy working their day jobs to randomly find diamonds in the rough. Sure, it does happen occasionally. But, most of the time, they're dealing with people who are taking the initiative to actually reach out to them (or the agents those people worked hard to impress).

Be aware that many times when you ask for something, the answer is going to be "no." This is, I believe, why so many people don't even ask to begin with. We've gotten too used to accepting rejection because we've heard the word "no" too many times. And, let's face it, rejection hurts. As a result, we learned that it's best not to ask for something in the first place.

However, this is a bad pattern of thinking. If you ask for something you want, perhaps the odds of a "no" answer are fifty percent. Maybe for something big the odds against receiving it are ninety percent. However, if you don't ask to begin with, the odds for a "no" are one hundred percent (unless the person is a mind reader). By asking, you at least have a *chance* to get what you want.

In a former teaching job, a colleague asked for more money when he signed a new contract, even though he had heard, like me, that the administration rarely granted these requests. I'll never know what answer he received, but I give him credit for at least trying. After all, if he had to live with a lower paycheck, at least he could sleep at night knowing that he made an effort to make more money. I had to live with a low paycheck knowing that I made no effort to raise it.

As a teen wanting to be popular, you must learn to ask, ask, and ask. If you have a need, ask for it. Heck, even if you have a want, ask for it. It could be as simple as a free refill for your drink at Starbucks, or as "complicated" as a new car for your sixteenth birthday. The first rule is that if you don't ask, you'll never receive. The same is true of being popular. If you want the benefits that come from popularity, then ask for them.

You may be thinking how the world is against you and no one

ever says "yes" to you. One of the reasons so many people hear "no" all the time (perhaps this is you) is because of the way they ask the question. They are whiny, mean, or demanding. I had students who'd ask a question and if I said "no," even in a nice way, would mutter something under their breath and walk away to show their displeasure. Let's just say with that response I wasn't likely to grant any of their requests in the future, even the reasonable ones.

A popular person, however, will use humor, build rapport, and find other techniques to make the odds of "yes" a little better. Even if people have to tell you "no," if you're mature and friendly, the odds of them giving you at least something or making a compromise with you increase.

I had a student ask me once if she could have extra credit for the semester. I told her "no" because it was against department policy. She was so kind and respectful, however, that I offered instead to help her prepare for the remaining tests – on my own time. I wanted to help her because of the kind and genuine way she talked to me. You'll find this open attitude among many of your teachers, and even among your parents.

Sometimes, however, you'll still hear "no" even if you've done everything right. Once, I asked an employee at McDonald's for a free refill on their iced coffee. I was friendly, funny, and even built rapport with the girl. But, I heard the word "no." Giving refills on iced coffee was against company policy and she probably didn't want to get in trouble, even for a funny and charming customer like me. It wasn't the end of the world. I survived. But, it didn't stop me from asking another employee the next day. He was more willing to bend the rules and I got my refill.

Whenever you ask for something, you have to be prepared for a negative answer. How do you take it? First, you are detached (Chapter 12). Second, there's no failure, only feedback (Chapter 11). Also, the answer may have nothing to do with you. In my case, maybe the girl at the register had given free drinks to her friends in the past and her manager had been watching her like a hawk. She also might just be a stickler for the rules (nothing wrong with that). Whatever the reason, it doesn't matter if you hear "no." Do like I did: try again later or pick another person to ask.

Keep in mind that someone who asks for stuff all the time becomes viewed as a sponge. I had a friend in high school who always called me for rides. He never offered gas money and would ask me to take him to events where I wasn't even invited. You never want people to think you are a mooch.

This is why it's essential that you internalize the "give-get-give" mindset (see Chapter 10). If you've given a lot to others (in the form of time, humor, talents, etc.) then they will gladly give to you, out of a sense of generosity, not because they want to shut up the mooch. If you have to rely on other people due to your circumstances in life, then be generous in any way you can, like offering to pay for gas when possible or maybe buying your ride's lunch when you're out.

Your assignment for this chapter is to practice asking for things. Come up with a few things that you'd really like to have, no matter how big or small. You can ask for anything, even extra French fries from the lunch ladies. Even if you just *know* you'll get a negative answer, write down what you want anyway. In fact, make sure to pick at least one item that is very "unrealistic" (but that you can still reasonably request from someone).

Next, go out and ask others to give you what you wrote on your list. You can try this at school, home, work, or anywhere. Make sure the person you ask has the ability to give you what you want. For example, if you want eighty dollars for new boots, ask someone who could realistically afford to give you that kind of money (and would be expected to do so).

I want you to notice two things. First, hearing the word "no" won't kill you, and second, the answer won't even be "no" that often. You'll be amazed how flexible other people can be when asked nicely and with a sense of humor. So, when you ask, use all of the skills you've learned so far in the book's other chapters.

Chapter 23

Have A Little Mystery

I went to school with a young lady who was extremely outgoing, almost to the point of being an absolute open book. If she had something on her mind, she said it. Even if you just met her, you'd get her life story after five minutes. She was fun to be around at first, but after a while most people lost interest. She was so open, there was no sense of mystery and no joy of discovery. Her friends could only hear about her difficult "time of the month" so many mornings before seeking conversation with someone a little less open.

If you want to be popular, it's important that you don't make the mistake of this young lady. Try to keep a certain air of mystery about you. Don't lie about yourself or get others to think you're something you're obviously not. However, you also don't want to give away too much information all at once. The brain actually enjoys figuring out missing pieces of the puzzle. It's why humans love trivia, challenges, corn mazes, etc. Imagine watching a trivia game show if it was just a bunch of facts listed for thirty minutes. Game shows are popular because they keep the audience in suspense and working hard to try to figure out the solution to hidden problems.

Let me give you an example about mystery in action from my life. At one coffee shop where I spent a lot of time, a young woman who worked there was always interested in what I did for a living. I was intentionally vague, so she would constantly guess about my career and status. Because I brought books with me, she assumed I was a writer. I told her "yes, I write" (I may have even worked on this book that day). I once wore a shirt with a map of Japan on it and she asked if I'd ever been to Japan. I told her jokingly, "I'm big in Japan." Another time she asked if I was famous. I told her, "Of course, everyone here loves me, don't they?"

See how I didn't really answer any of her questions. As frustrating as it may have been for her, I did it on purpose. And, I might add, it had its desired effect. Every time I refused to answer, you notice how she tried to fill in the blanks about me? She knew I was high-value by the way I acted and talked, so she naturally wanted to figure out why and how I'd become so attractive and popular. By refusing to be direct, I only increased her desire to know more about me (and continue to give me attention).

As you become popular, you can benefit from the brain's preference for mystery. It's like when I was in second grade and a new girl came into my class. I remember being so excited by the mystery of a new student, I can recall desperately trying to get a glimpse of her at the bus stop. As I got to know her, I found out she wasn't anything special. But, when she was new and mysterious, my brain found her so fascinating. It even tried to fill in the blanks. Was she cute? Did she enjoy playing the same games I played? Was her house nice? Of course, my brain assumed the answer was "yes" to all of these questions.

In order to create an air of mystery, you'll have to follow two basic pieces of advice. The first is not to tell every single detail about yourself. This can actually be helpful when you're meeting new people because you may not be the most exciting or awesome person in the world right now.

I did this a lot when I was starting my business. I told people I was starting a business and they'd ask what it was all about. I'd say, "What doesn't it do?" laugh, and leave it at that. What I didn't say was that I had just started my business and was in the process of building it. Now that I'm more established and successful, I'm more direct. But, in the beginning, my responses allowed me to appear mysterious and keep me from having to explain that my business was my colleagues and I working our butts off for a vague concept (popularity consultants).

My second tip is to do what I did with Stacy, the employee at the coffee shop. I got her to create a trans-derivational search, or TDS, about me. A TDS, a "Neuro-Linguistic Programming" concept, occurs when the person you're talking to tries to make sense of what you've just said. If you're direct and detailed, there's no need for a TDS.

However, if you're vague or elusive, you'll find your conversation partners doing a TDS to understand the meaning behind your words.

For example, if you ask your buddy, "Remember that feeling you had at school yesterday?" it will lead to a TDS while he determines what you were talking about. Was it the feeling of happiness when the hot girl in science class smiled at him, or the feeling of frustration when he found out that he failed his math test? Purposefully creating a TDS forces a person to pause and think, which interrupts his or her normal thought patterns. This puts people in a trance-like state and makes them open to suggestion and interaction with you. Signs of a TDS are a pause, wide eyes, dilated pupils, slight confusion, etc. You may see this frequently when you talk about "teenage stuff" to your parents.

If you want to create a TDS with someone, it's not hard. The best way is to be ambiguous. This is when you say words that can be taken in multiple ways. For example, if I say, "The woman stabbed the boy with an umbrella," it can mean different things. It could mean a woman stabbed a boy who was holding an umbrella, or a woman used an umbrella as a weapon to stab the boy.

If you recall my earlier story, I used ambiguity with Stacy successfully. For example, by telling her, "I'm big in Japan" she had to wonder whether I was kidding and, even if I wasn't, what does being "big in Japan" mean anyway? A direct answer would've been, "My wife bought this shirt for me at the airport during a stopover in Japan as a present." However, that doesn't sound nearly as cool, does it? And, the direct answer wouldn't get her terribly excited about knowing more about me either.

Why would you want to get someone to create a trans-derivational search? Ultimately you want to generate a TDS to get others to fill in the blanks about you in a positive way. While I'm a cool, popular, and successful (and modest, right?) guy, when I let Stacy create a version of me in her mind, I guarantee what she came up with was far superior to even my great reality. She made positive assumptions about me and viewed me even more highly afterward.

Still, you don't just want to just play with someone's mind, as entertaining as that may sound. You ultimately want to get each person to assume something positive or mysterious about you. For example, if you walk into a place and say, "This would be a cool place for my band to play" people are going to assume that you're in a band. Maybe you are, and your band sucks. However, people will hear "band" and probably, unless they're overly familiar with crappy bands, fill in the blanks in a positive fashion. They may ask themselves, "What kind of band is he in?" "Is he famous?" and so on.

A TDS is typically formed positively or negatively based on the mood or situation of the people you're talking to. This makes sense if you think about it. They are not basing their opinion of you on actual facts, but on their own assumptions about who they think you are (or want you to be). If they're happy and in a good mood, they're likely to assume good things. This is even truer if you're the one who has put them in a good mood. So, make sure you've shown your sense of humor and high-value before trying to generate a TDS. Then they'll assume the best about you.

Keep in mind that while mystery is important, there are times when being mysterious or vague isn't appropriate. If you're responding to a question from a teacher and you're vague and elusive, you may flunk the test. Also, you don't want to be so ambiguous that people think you're weird. Use common sense about when to be mysterious and when to be more straightforward. You also don't want to have such an air of mystery about you that others begin to think you're a snob. You want to give of yourself to others; just do it slowly and in a way that still preserves some mystery.

I give the advice in this chapter to my adult clients and it's typically successful. However, being a teen you'll probably have more challenges. The first is that most of your time is spent in school and at most schools everyone knows your business, from the time you struck out during the crucial baseball game at twelve, to how you were dumped by the foreign exchange student last week. In other words, in your normal environment mystery may hard to come by.

While you can easily project an air of mystery around people you meet outside of school (or change schools), it is still possible to create a little mystery in the school where you've spent most of your life. Hopefully since you've been reading this book, you have been changing: how you act, look, carry yourself, etc. If you've been putting real effort into your changes, I'm sure others have been noticing. When they try to find out the reasons for your changes, give them some mystery. A good response is, "It's all about the fame and fortune."

This response is vague, but still the truth. You are becoming more popular (fame) and are learning skills that will help you earn more money (fortune). If they press you further, tell them you're trying to improve yourself. You might even recommend this book if you think they'll benefit from it, and won't make fun of you for seeking popularity advice.

Your assignment for this chapter is to write down ways that you can be more mysterious on a regular basis. Then, put those goals into practice. Remember, the purpose isn't to lie or mislead, just to create ambiguity. Look at my examples throughout the chapter for ways to be more mysterious. Also, the best way to be more mysterious instantly is to simply not talk about yourself in great detail around others so much. No one really wants to hear your life story all the time anyway.

CHAPTER 24

CREEPY IS NEVER POPULAR

A guy I knew growing up had a lot of the traits that I've mentioned in this book. He was outgoing, charming, intelligent, and even funny at times. Of course, he also told a girl who started liking him that he had fantasies about killing other people so he could impress her. Let's just say, in spite of his other social assets, his photo was always next to the words "perpetually single" in the dictionary.

This guy, like many people out there, was creepy. And, let me tell you, being creepy is always a deal-breaker when it comes to popularity. Always. I'll say (or write) it one more time: being creepy is always a deal breaker when it comes to popularity. If you're creepy, you might as well flush your dreams of becoming popular down the crapper, no matter your other skills.

Being creepy means you create an uneasy feeling in other people.

It isn't just what you say that can be creepy. The way you look, your mannerisms, body language, dress, gestures, etc. can also make other people feel nervous around you.

It's hard to put a specific definition on what makes someone creepy, but we usually know it when we see it. As humans, our brains are wired to keep us safe. My hypothesis is that when a guy "creeps you out" (and it usually is a guy) you are subconsciously picking up body language cues and other signals that the creepy person may be dangerous. Since this happens subconsciously, this explains why usually you can't even vocalize why a person strikes you as a creep. Most "creepers" aren't actually dangerous, but they unknowingly send out signals that they could be.

I knew a guy in college who was good-looking and whose family had money. But, he constantly talked about death when he went out to meet new people. He thought he did it in a "philosophical" manner, which, in his mind, made it acceptable. Everyone else didn't see it that way, since he rarely made any new friends on his outings and actually lost old friends who became really tired of his constant creepy talk.

Although I don't think he ended up hurting or killing anyone, he definitely came across as a potential serial killer. And, since survival is the number one goal of every species (*homo sapiens* included), hanging out with potential serial killers isn't at the top of any one's "to do" list.

Since you may have been creepy your entire life (drawing dead people in kindergarten anyone?), being non-creepy may require work.

But like every other problem you face in this book, overcoming it is not insurmountable. The first step is to become self-aware. You must be able to understand your thoughts, actions, and how your thoughts influence your actions. I've written an entire chapter on this that should offer additional help (Chapter 25).

Second, get some feedback from friends and act on it. I'm sure your friends can tell you if other people think you're creepy. If you have no friends to tell you, then that's a red flag that you're certainly creepy. Also, go out with some guys or girls that you know are not creepy (hint: if they have a lot of friends, they probably aren't creepy) and have them examine how you interact with people. If they see anything creepy, have them tell you (privately). If you're truly creepy, you likely don't even know that what you're doing is inappropriate.

Some creepy behavior may be accidental, like an off-hand comment or gesture, but other things you do and say might be regular creepy occurrences, and it is important that you know it. You can also act like your non-creepy friends. Watch what they say, and more specifically, what they don't say. The difference between charming and creepy usually hinges on what is *not* said. Creepy people often lack "filters." We all have inappropriate thoughts, but creepy people actually share them in public settings.

Keep in mind that a few topics typically make most people uncomfortable: death, violence, mental illness, rape, bizarre interests like the occult, and odd sexual preferences. If you're too young to see it on a movie screen, or you have to be twenty-one to learn more about it on the internet, it's best to avoid it in public conversation, especially when dealing with total strangers.

Finally, change creepy behavior. If you're going to succeed, you'll have to learn to self-censor and discard old behavior patterns. Develop your filter. If you think your actions or comments will make someone feel weird or uncomfortable enough to want to stop being around you, keep your weirdness hidden in your innermost thoughts. Otherwise you'll possess a bunch of positive traits, but one seemingly small hindrance will make them all pointless. Your brain can be re-wired (see Chapter 3) and you'll have to get those non-creepy neurons firing.

If you fail the "creepy test," your homework is to write out a plan to stop being creepy, based on my tips in this chapter. If you believe you need some extra help "de-creeping," but don't know where to start, keep reading this book and applying the advice in your life. This will help you shed the "creep" label.

David has written three detailed articles on our website that will help you learn more about creepiness, determine if you (or your child) is creepy, and finally, how to successfully stop being so creepy. Check them out:

thepopularteen.com/dont-be-creeper-creepy-the-rule

thepopularteen.com/four-ways-to-know-if-you-are-a-creepy-creeper

thepopularteen.com/how-to-stop-being-creepy-and-become-popular

CHAPTER 25

YOUR PARENTS WERE RIGHT: PAY ATTENTION

I was taking the daughter of a family friend home from school one day and we passed the flashing yellow lights at an intersection where she lived. She was in a hurry and told me to hit the gas before the lights turned red. I laughed and told her that those lights never turn red. They're always blinking yellow, and have for the nearly fourteen years she'd lived on that road! She gave me a funny look and started laughing. She admitted she'd never noticed before. I asked her how long it was until she started driving. When she said "two years," I breathed a small sigh of relief.

As I mentioned when I talked about mindfulness in Chapter 12, most people go through life in a barely-aware state. Just like the young family friend, they can even live or go to school in a place for years and barely notice any of the details. It's sad, but most humans are unconcerned with their surroundings or even with their own mental state. Lack of awareness doesn't just make you less popular. Think about all the problems that could be prevented if everyone simply paid more attention: medical errors, car accidents, late arrivals, failed tests, etc.

A Buddhist monk once asked his teacher to write down the fundamental teaching of Buddhism. The master wrote "attention" on the piece of paper. The student disliked the answer, thinking the answer had to be more complex. He bugged the teacher for a while and the teacher finally gave in and elaborated. He wrote, "attention, attention, attention."

I love this story because I truly believe that success in life, whether it's making money, being a good parent, succeeding in a job, or attaining popularity at school, is mostly about paying attention. You pay attention to the world around you and you can anticipate needs and problems. You pay attention to people and you can learn the ways to win them over and get them to do what you want (including becoming your friend or romantic partner). You pay attention to details and you will always be able to outsmart the rest of the world.

For someone wanting to be popular, paying attention is key. Look at the example I gave in Chapter 20 when I discussed the origins of rock-and-roll music. Not only were the early pioneers of rock music breaking from the herd, they were paying attention to the large number of people who hated the current music. Every popular person, whether he or she is aware of it or not, is great at paying attention. From being aware of what traits people want in a friend, to the skills it takes to be popular in modern high schools, popularity involves seeing a need and meeting it.

Another reason why paying attention is so valuable is due to a sad fact of modern life: most people don't get as much attention as they need. This is especially true with teens. A large number of them today were raised without both parents, have a father or mother (or both) who work long hours and are rarely seen, spent most of their time in daycare growing up, and so forth. It's a safe bet that most of your classmates (and maybe even you) aren't getting the attention they crave.

I witnessed it all the time as a teacher. Many of my students were so hungry for attention that they spent their study halls getting passes to come talk to me. While I was happy to give of my time, you know young people are hungry for attention when they willingly use their free time to hang out with a teacher.

You can capitalize on the loneliness epidemic that is crushing the youth of America. By taking an interest in people, actively listening to them, and giving them your attention, they will then value you because you're meeting one of their core needs.

So, even though you are going out and dealing with generally lonely people, don't let anyone give you any crap about "exploiting" them. You're not taking advantage of anyone. You are focusing on making genuine friendships, and meeting someone else's needs (having someone pay attention to them) and they, in turn, are meeting needs of yours (making you more popular and paying attention to you). Everyone wins.

Another reason why you must learn to pay attention if you want to be popular is that it makes you look extremely high-value. A lot of what makes people appear talented is really just the art of paying attention. If you do well in school, it's because you pay attention to what you're learning. If you're a great actor, it's because you've paid attention so well in real life that you can effectively model it on the screen and stage. A really funny person pays attention to what gets the most laughs and provides that type of humor to others. You get it? If not, pay attention.

Whenever I go out and meet people, my paying attention skills are always on display and help me become more and more popular. Let me give you an outline of a typical encounter.

When I enter a place, I pay attention to body language, so I approach people who seem open to interaction with me (unless I'm in a particular daring mood). When I talk to these strangers, I use observational humor related to details in the environment or from current events (more paying attention). If it's a girl, I tease her a little about some detail of her clothing. Finally, I read the situation to determine if the person is interested enough for me to ask for his or her contact information.

You see how my whole evening was spent paying attention? My

success started with paying attention, continued with paying attention, and ended by paying attention. In fact, this entire book comes from techniques I've developed, learned, and mastered throughout my entire life. I paid attention to what people needed, then further paid attention to what worked and what didn't. It's like the Buddhist master said: "attention, attention, attention."

Your homework is to re-read all of Chapter 12 and re-do that homework. I'm guessing that you're not as mindful or detached as you should be. Mindfulness and detachment are both necessary to pay attention properly. This is because if you're preoccupied or living in the past or future, you'll never be able to truly pay attention in the present and use that skill to become more popular.

The second part of your assignment is to really pay attention to three people tomorrow. Find individuals you think need another person's attention and/or whom you'd like to befriend or possibly date. However, don't be creepy or act like their counselor. This is meant to get to know new people by meeting their needs for attention, not a chance for you to try out your amateur psychologist skills. Also, write down observations about them you noticed from paying attention.

CHAPTER 26

POPULARITY IS ALL ABOUT RELATIONSHIPS

I love social networking websites and apps. They're great places to reconnect with old friends and connect with new ones. Sure, the whiny status updates and drama can be a little annoying, but the possibilities for making friends and connections are pretty much endless. However, one of my former students recently de-friended me on Facebook. At first I wondered what I'd done, but then realized that her first week of college, she deleted everyone from her high school, including her former classmates and teachers.

About six weeks after she deleted me, I saw her mom when I was having coffee. Her mom told me how she was struggling at school and was thinking of transferring to a college closer to home. She wondered if I would write her daughter a letter of recommendation. I told her mom I'd be happy to do it, so long as her daughter took the initiative and asked me herself. Needless to say I never heard anything.

When my dad was negotiating a property deal to expand his non-profit, he ran into some problems with a real estate agent on the building he wanted to buy. When dad realized that the warehouse was owned by a local businessman whom he knew well, he made a phone call. The problem was fixed. When a shocked employee of the non-profit told dad she was surprised he'd solved the issue with so little effort, dad laughed and told her, "It's all about relationships."

Those words have stuck with me throughout the years. Dad makes great efforts to start and nurture positive relationships and finds great financial and social success from such a mentality. My (former Facebook) friend, on the other hand, decided to burn a bunch of bridges and is still struggling academically and in other ways. I wonder why.

There's an old saying that states: "it's not *what* you know, but *who* you know." This statement has always been true, but with the popularity of social media apps and text messaging, it is truer than ever. Why do you think people become popular? It's because they make the right impressions upon a large number of people. I promise you there is not a celebrity or popular individual alive who has not gotten a break by knowing someone with connections. For example, Kris Kristofferson (ask your grandparents about him), a famous musician and actor, was a janitor at a recording studio before he made it big in music. Did he spend his time *just* cleaning toilets? I doubt it.

Relationships make life more enjoyable.

The best way to benefit from relationships, socially and otherwise, is to create new ones and make an effort to maintain the ones you have. You can follow the tips laid out later in this book to approach, build rapport, and then make the close to expand your social circle (Chapters 35, 36, and 37).

But, to maintain the friends you have, the best method is to – surprise – pay attention to them on a regular basis. My good friend Joshua Wagner likes to interact with at least five people a day on social media. Another tip would be to call or text at least one friend from your contact list daily, especially one whom you usually wouldn't interact with. Whatever option you choose, what matters most is that you make an effort to keep up with your friendships and other connections on a regular basis.

Another tip is to never, ever, discount the smaller connections you've made. Once I was having a conversation with an acquaintance who asked how many Facebook friends I had. When I told him over a thousand, he snickered and launched into a lecture on how no one can really have that many friends. He's not alone. Most people would mock the idea that one human being can have over a thousand friends.

They're wrong. It's true that no one can reasonably have that many deep and intimate friendships. However, from a networking standpoint, having that many connections is an incredible blessing. When I launch a new website, I have over a thousand potential "likes" from the start. When I start to promote a new book, it's automatically exposed to over a thousand people before it's even released. And, to forget about business for a while, from a purely pleasure standpoint, I enjoy interacting with a variety of people on a regular basis. Not a bad deal.

A few months ago, a woman I know deactivated her Facebook account because her husband asked her to. It limited her world considerably. Rather than having access to her previous five hundred contacts, she now has pretty much her husband. While he's fairly successful, he doesn't have the contacts and opportunities of five hundred people. If someone on her list has a party, wants to give away free concert tickets, or needs an extra for his upcoming YouTube comedy sketch, guess who's going to miss out?

That's why I always tell my clients, especially teens, that unless you're being harassed, don't delete contacts from your phone or your social networking circle. Also, resist the urge to leave a social network just because your friends decide to leave. For example, right now teens are leaving Facebook for Twitter and Instagram. I spend more time on these two networks now too. However, many people are still on Facebook and use it regularly. You don't have to be on there all the time, but maintaining a basic presence is a good idea for networking.

Why should you stay in touch with as many people as possible? You never know when even the smallest opportunity could pay off. I've gotten a graphic designer, content writers, and models for my websites and books from my social networking contacts.

I want to end this chapter by telling you a little more about my dad and the benefits he receives from forging close friendships with other people, especially men and women in high places. His agency gets constant referrals from networking contacts. If he needs anything, he can almost always make a phone call and get it. If he runs into problems, he knows the right person to contact to get it resolved immediately. I remember as a child traveling to Wisconsin and having the sheriff tell dad to call day or night if he ran into any issues. That impressed me.

Of course, dad knows it's about relationships, since I got that advice from him. He is in the helping industry so he's counseled and advised countless people, their cousins, aunts, uncles, sons, daughters, best friends, etc. People also know if they call him for a problem that he can solve, he will do his best to solve it. So, my dad truly understands that it's about "give-get-give" in relationships, not just about getting his own way all of the time. Remember, when you meet the needs of others, they have a strong desire to help you in return, in whatever way they can.

Your assignment is to interact with five friends (including adults) on your social networks right now. It only takes a few minutes, so you should make a habit of doing this each day. The more you interact with your contacts, even in small ways, the more likely they will think of you when they have opportunities or help you if the time comes.

If you don't have a Facebook, Twitter, or other social media account, and you're old enough (and your parents allow it), get one. If you deactivated your account, then bring it back from the dead. Popularity today requires relationships, both real and virtual.

CHAPTER 27

ASSERT YOURSELF

My teaching techniques and methods, although effective and extremely popular, were never fully embraced by the more traditional administrators at the school where I taught. I was a maverick, to say the least. Consequently, one spring the administration decided to not renew my contract for the next year.

However, my popularity was such that during one of the daily morning convocations, the entire student body participated in a sit-in to protest my dismissal. After the concluding remarks by the student leaders, the entire student body, with a few exceptions, remained seated and refused to leave. One girl, sitting on the end of the row of seats, was even specifically asked by the dean of students to leave. She politely, but firmly, refused.

What the students did that day was almost universally admired, not only by their friends from other schools, but also by their parents and many of their teachers. The girl who respectfully defied the dean was even later praised for her brave actions – by the dean himself!

Right now, you likely are feeling respect for my former students too, because they stood up to those in power for a cause they deeply believed in. I know this because being assertive is almost universally considered a high-value trait. If you look around, you can see this in action. For example, kids at your school who stand up to bullies, take the lead on the sports field, and speak their mind to teachers are probably admired, at least for those traits. We like assertive individuals because they often say (and do) what we feel we cannot.

The vast majority of students and parents opposed my dismissal. But, it took a handful of assertive student leaders to stand up for me by organizing and executing a successful protest. Even throughout history, our heroes have tended to be strong leaders like Gandhi, Martin Luther King, Jr., and other brave men and women who asserted themselves when others who may have agreed with them remained quiet.

There are a variety of reasons why individuals do not assert themselves more often. First, a lot of people, especially teenagers, think that being assertive is the same as being mean. So, they don't speak up for fear of offending other people. Second, there are those who fear asserting themselves because they are afraid of the consequences. This is especially true of teens because school environments often discourage speaking up for yourself. Sadly, some teachers don't even accept respectful and thoughtful disagreement.

If you want to be assertive, you'll not only have to stop being passive (which should be obvious), but you'll also have to avoid the other extreme on the spectrum: aggression. Unfortunately, especially in high schools, a lot of people skip assertiveness and go straight into aggression. Aggression doesn't even have to be physical violence. There are emotional, mental, and other types of violence too.

Basically, when you stand up for your opinion, if it is done in a way that harms others, then you've passed into aggression. This can include putting others down, using sarcasm, yelling, bullying, violating personal space, etc. Aggression isn't just jerk behavior; it's also ineffective in the long-term. Aggressive people may get their way in the short-term. However, in the long-term being aggressive causes people to resent and distrust you. This isn't a good strategy for popularity.

Another type of behavior to avoid is being passive-aggressive. This is when you have an aggressive intent, but express it indirectly or passively.

For example, let's say someone takes your seat at lunch after you've put your tray down. A passive person would just move his tray. An aggressive person might threaten or use violence. A passive-aggressive person would say something like, "This school has so many idiots who can't tell when a seat has already been taken." The comment is clearly aggressive in tone, but is delivered in a way that isn't directly violent or menacing. A passive-aggressive person might also stay silent during the incident (passivity), but sneakily gossip about the seat-stealer later (aggression).

Passive-aggressive behavior is usually looked down upon because it shows weakness. It tells the world you are angry and *want* to deal with an issue, but you don't have the confidence to directly confront it. It is also sneaky and back-biting behavior, which nobody likes. Avoid being passive-aggressive at all costs, especially if you're a guy.

So, if you want to be high-value, you'll have to avoid the traps of being passive, aggressive, or passive-aggressive. You'll need to master the fourth option: assertiveness. The tips below will allow you to assert yourself without being a jerk. They'll help you become admired and popular too.

First, always make sure you're relaxed and detached (see Chapter 12). Even if you fear consequences like getting punished or beaten up, you must act like you don't. You have to be seen as cool, calm, and relaxed. If others think you're operating from fear or anger, they'll likely see you as a reactor, not a leader.

Second, avoid the language and action of judgment. This is much easier when you're detached and relaxed. When you assert yourself in any situation, this is extremely important. Very few people respond to being judged. Observing is much more helpful than judging. For example, let's say you want to express dissatisfaction to a teacher. Instead of saying, "You are a mean witch (or worse!)," you might say, "I don't think your last punishment was fair because..." The minute you call someone a name, they will stop listening to what you have to say.

Observation always beats judgment if you want people to listen to you. So, stick to your own opinions and needs without belittling or judging others. In fact, it's best to avoid "you" statements altogether because saying "you" frequently in a conversation with other people comes across as judgmental, especially in more stressful situations.

Third, try to empathize with the other people involved. Empathy is the ability to understand and share the feelings of another, that is, to know where they are coming from. This is related to the lack of judgmentalism. While people make boneheaded decisions, in most cases when you need to assert yourself, the individuals in question aren't trying to be evil. In fact, they may have some of the same difficulties that you are having. It's helpful to try to understand the motivation behind another person's behavior and then express that empathy when you assert yourself.

To show empathy, you can use "I understand you feel [upset, frustrated, or other emotions]" to begin your conversation. This is where you acknowledge the person's feelings, so they don't think you're attacking them.

Fourth, when you assert yourself, try to offer something of value to the other person. When we feel we're "losing" an argument, we dig in our heels and get defensive. Yet, if we feel like we're being understood and getting something out of a deal, we're more likely to get on board. So, when you stand up to someone or have to be assertive, offer some type of compromise. Below are a few examples of how to be assertive with empathy, non-judgment, and compromise.

Scenario - The person next to you is talking during a class lecture.

Wrong response - "Can't you just shut up? I'm failing this class!"

Right response - "I really need to pass this test and these notes could be important. Could you either whisper or pass notes instead?"

Observations - Notice how the correct response focuses on the need to pass a test and lacks harsh language and judgment? Also, it gives a reasonable alternative so both sides can be happy.

Scenario - Your teacher seems to be singling you out for punishment.

Wrong response - "I don't know why you have to pick on me all the time. I'm not the only one acting out, you know!"

Right response - "I know this class can be difficult and I'm hardly innocent. But, lately I've felt frustrated because it seems like you've been singling me out for special punishment. If I'm doing something I'm not aware of, I'll gladly try to improve my behavior."

Observation - The first response is really a reaction of frustration, which will likely just make the teacher mad. The correct response shows deliberate thought and maturity. It also recognizes the stress the class likely brings to the teacher, takes some personal responsibility for it, and offers a role in helping to make it better.

Another part of being assertive is learning to say "no." For whatever reason, a lot of people have a hard time doing this. It could be a desire to please others or maybe a fear that saying "no" could result in a loss of a relationship. However, not being able to say "no" often causes great stress. Usually people who can't say "no" are given more and more responsibilities until they feel like going crazy! Don't let that be you.

Learning how to say "no" is also a bit of an art. All of the tips in this chapter will help you say "no" correctly. However, here is some specific advice you will find helpful.

The first thing to remember when saying "no" is to recall the reason why you're being asked to do something. In most cases, you are being asked because you are good at what you do or because the person asking has a real need.

When I worked a summer job at Kmart, I used to get upset when I would be called about taking extra hours. Now I realize I received calls because I was a good employee and the manager needed coverage for the store (and her job) to function properly. I still would've said "no" in many cases, but my perspective certainly would've been better.

Second, when you say "no," do it with non-judgment, empathy, and compromise like mentioned previously. Typically, it's helpful to thank others for thinking of you. Then, if possible, offer a way to help them meet their needs, or put them in contact with someone who can. If you tell people "no" in ways that are snarky or negative, they won't want to follow you or be around you much, which is unpopularity. Below I've given a few examples of how to say "no" properly.

Scenario - A teacher needs your help after school with a club activity, but you need some alone time.

Wrong response - "I'm busy, but sure."

Right response - "Thanks for thinking of me, but I have been so busy that tonight I just need a break. I'd be happy to help you another time, and maybe even drag some friends along."

Observation - The first response is wrong because it is clearly not what the person really wants. The second answer, however, shows gratitude for the offer and then a willingness to do it: at a later time and with some help. Both of those are reasonable requests a teacher will likely respect, so long as the activity doesn't have to be done right away.

Scenario - A friend always asks for a ride, but the last five times has never offered gas money.

Wrong response - "Can't you ever just get another ride?"

Right response - "I understand you need a ride, but gas is expensive and you live out of the way. I'll take you, but would really appreciate a contribution every now and then."

Observation - The first response is wrong because it's a reaction and dismissive. By being understanding about his needs and honest about your finances, you are giving empathy and setting yourself up to receive some in return. Not only that, but you're "compromising" by reminding him that you live out of the way and are doing him a favor. You're also not asking for tons of money, just a small contribution on a regular basis, which he can likely give you.

So, try to be more assertive in your life in all environments. People may be shocked at first if they're used to your passivity, but if you stand up in ways that are respectful using the tips outlined in this chapter, they will ultimately value you and respect you more.

For homework, write down five ways in which you'd like to assert yourself. Make them specific. You likely know where you need to be less passive. It could be as mundane as to assert yourself when a restaurant messes up your order, or as large as demanding that a bully leave you alone. Whatever you pick, next write an action plan with steps and/or conversations that are empathetic, non-judgmental, and show some compromise. Finally, resolve to carry out the plan soon. No one likes a doormat (and it's bad for your mental health).

For more information about communicating, check out "Non-Violent Communication," a system developed by psychologist Marshall Rosenberg. Many of this chapter's concepts are based on this system. See the Recommended Reading section for more resources.

CHAPTER 28

BE ONLINE AND STILL BE EXCELLENT

I am friends with a college acquaintance on Facebook whose wall posts are incredibly whiny. So, she'll post something like "Jane is sooooooo fake," and Jane will jump into the conversation, and it turns into a back-and-forth of nasty put-downs and bitterness. Let's just say that this woman's wall is mostly filled with posts by herself and others that are whiny or related to starting trouble. And, keep in mind, she's not a teenager, but a thirty-something woman!

On the other hand, my friend Joshua Wagner and co-author David Bennett have awesome Facebook walls. They never whine or post overly personal revelations, but give the world funny (and original) status updates, which their friends regularly comment on. They have a lot of Facebook friends, and their walls are popular places to "virtually" hang out and find inspiration and laughter.

You can be cool, even while online.

I've mentioned throughout the book how to use social media to become popular. And, the more popular you become in real life, the more people will want to connect with you online. Social media is quickly becoming the primary way to stay in contact, not just for teenagers, but also for adults. That may explain why your mom is on Facebook more than you. However, if you don't have an online presence in today's United States of America, your popularity (and general success) potential is quite small.

Sadly, some people who are cool in real life think that when they get online they can be creepy, rude, whiny, or a host of other unattractive traits, all because they don't have to actually deal with another human being in person. In fact, online drama among young people is so common that colleges and companies are checking out the social media posts of future students and employees.

I've taught students who either missed out on college opportunities, or nearly did, because of their raunchy and inappropriate social media use. Yep, the schools found out. In addition, law enforcement is starting to get involved since online bullying has become a problem at many high schools.

The moral of the story is that if you want to be popular, you can't do everything right at school and your job, but be an annoying loser online. You have to create a cool online persona that matches the cool real-life (hopefully) you. It's not just adults in positions of power that are monitoring your social media presence. Your friends, friends of friends, acquaintances, etc. are too, but for more social reasons. Do your wall posts, feeds, interactions, pictures, videos, likes, and groups say "friend/follow me" or "defriend/unfollow me?"

Make sure you follow the advice in this book whenever you're online. In other words, be flexible, fun, detached, funny, etc., not only when you see people in person, but also when you interact with them on your wall or feed, through text messages, and so on. Remember to be patient too, since lots of teens (and adults) think being online gives them permission to act differently. Don't get sucked into their drama (see Chapter 19).

Here are a few tips for behaving online. Follow them and you will be successful on the internet and social media.

Don't put yourself down, because it makes you look low-value, unless it is an obvious joke (like a football lineman joking about being too skinny).

If you're a guy, don't act like a girl, or broadcast your love for girly things. Look at the types of things your female friends say, and how they say it, and don't imitate them. You might think sharing your love for Twilight will impress girls. Nope. It'll just keep you in "the friend zone," since they will see you as "one of the girls."

Don't broadcast your failures. Don't be the guy who advertises when he experiences romantic rejection, or the girl who is always whining about being single. Keep it to yourself or you will have more lost friends to whine about.

Don't be too political, religious, fanatical, etc. You don't have to be bland, but you don't want to be the person everybody ignores because every post is about how all meat-eaters are murderers, or how horribly unfair the world is to Justin Bieber.

Don't be online all the time. Show the world that you are successful, have hobbies, etc., outside of watching a screen refresh. Take a break from social media occasionally (unannounced) for a few moments (or even days) so everyone knows you have a life.

Don't say weird, sexual, or violent things. Don't talk about pornography, killing things (except legal hunting), bodily functions, your hatred of women or men, etc.

Don't play games all day or constantly repost/retweet someone else's pictures and statuses. Nothing says low-value like having a feed filled with game updates or photos and statuses you took from someone else while you were online all day. They suggest you don't have a social life (and you probably don't if you have time to play games and collect photos all day), and that you're unoriginal.

Don't be creepy (see Chapter 24). Don't add strangers as friends, or people you barely know, and don't "hover" around someone online, just as you wouldn't hover around them in public. This means you should take a break from liking every photo your crush posts, or responding to every tweet from that hot girl in Algebra II.

Don't whine, complain, or play the victim. The world is already too whiny. This will turn people away from you very quickly.

Don't overtly broadcast your successes (like by saying, "Can't believe I ran 10 miles today!"). Work it in indirectly or with humor. For example, say, "I really had to increase my pace on this morning's run thanks to the neighbor's Chihuahua chasing me!" Notice how it tells the world you're running while entertaining them.

Be funny and entertaining, but originally so. In other words, don't repeat other people's jokes. Most of your friends will be able to spot "canned" material a mile away.

Be friendly and encouraging to a diverse group of friends. Say "happy birthday," and "like," "favorite," and comment on a variety of people's statuses. However, change things up regularly, so you aren't stalking one or two profiles. In other words, keep as many people in your online loop as possible.

Write about diverse things. Be the one with multiple interests who is always doing and saying something new and exciting. This makes you attractive to a wide variety of people. For example, I write about working out, networking, my business, going out with family, sports, etc. Anyone following me can see that I am well-rounded with diverse tastes.

Be patient. Respond to follow requests, comments, etc., when you want to respond. There is no need to reply the minute or even day after, since you are successful and busy.

Know when to give up. Exit a fruitless, aggressive, or dumb discussion. There is no shame in bowing out if a discussion is beneath you. You may even wish to assertively make this known. It's probably best not to engage in these types of discussions to begin with.

Be mysterious. There is nothing wrong with being a little vague. Even if you aren't as successful or popular as you want to be, make people think you are. But, don't go so far as to lie. Eventually it will catch up with you (see Chapter 23).

Today your homework is to "revamp" your social media presence. If you have a blog or Tumblr with your real name attached to it, go and delete the obnoxious, creepy, or low-value posts. Go on your Facebook profile and edit your interests, jobs, inspiring figures, etc. to reflect the new high-value you. If your wall is filled with games, delete them. Better yet, stop playing and devote that time to nurturing talents or promoting yourself. You get the picture. Reboot your Facebook, Twitter, Instagram, Tumblr, etc. identity right now.

If you think you must whine, vent, or engage in pointless discussions, find a totally anonymous forum and let it loose. I would argue, however, that as you mature and grow as a person and become more popular, you will find little need to waste your time on such pointless nonsense.

CHAPTER 29

THE ROCK STAR PROBLEM (?)

When I was still involved in education, I was a popular and cool teacher. I enjoyed interacting with my students a lot. I won them over through a combination of my natural personality and the techniques in this book. They listened to me, respected me, and loved me. And, I might add, the feeling was mutual. I took great pride in my teenage students.

However, there were days when my free periods and my time before and after school were entirely taken up talking to students. Some of it was dealing with school-related issues, but most of it was simply hanging out. I enjoyed the time shooting the breeze with my students and appreciated the opportunity to mentor them. Yet, there were days when I had a lot to do, like grading or planning. During those times, while I was still honored to have all of the visitors, it

JONATHAN AND DAVID BENNETT

turned into a problem, one that we at *The Popular Teen* call the "Rock Star Problem (?)."

If you look carefully, you'll notice there's a question mark after the word "problem" in the title. After all, being popular is a blast, right? Sure it is or you wouldn't be reading this book. But I'd be lying if I said there wasn't a downside to being popular.

I don't want you to get the wrong idea; being popular is great and I believe that the more popular and confident people there are in the world, the better off we are. Still, I've included some of the most common problems you'll face as you become more popular so you'll have a realistic view of popularity's downside and be able to cope with it if it comes.

The first problem you may face is lack of privacy. The more people you know and interact with, the better the chances you will be noticed when you're in public. When I went to a county fair last year near my hometown, I was literally stopping every thirty seconds to talk to someone. I was thrilled to see many people I hadn't seen in a while and certainly felt honored to be liked. But, when I was dying of thirst and it took thirty minutes to make it one hundred yards to the iced tea stand because of conversations, I became frustrated.

You probably won't be mobbed at the cell phone store like a Hollywood celebrity. But, when you're popular, even in smaller environments like your school or neighborhood, you'll find that people want more of your time.

The second issue is what we call "celebrity gravity" (see Chapter 30). If you are popular, you will attract lots of people to you. In addition, they will sometimes compete for your attention, especially if you are scarce. You may find that when you're at parties, sporting events, or even out in public, people, and lots of them, will crowd you wanting your attention.

Now, if you're lonely, this may sound like a dream come true! Seeing this swarm effect in action is pretty cool, especially if you're the one being swarmed. However, if you're being swarmed by people when all you really want to do is chill, or you have something you need to accomplish quickly, you can see how it can turn into a problem.

Being attractive also means that some people will want your attention in more extreme ways. While being stalked isn't terribly common, it can happen. It's just something to be aware of, certainly not anything to worry about all the time. Obviously, if stalking or harassment becomes an issue, you should tell a teacher, your parents, another trusted adult, or directly contact the police themselves.

Finally, when people see your confidence and your success, they will want a piece of you. What this means will look different depending on your circumstances in life and level of popularity, but be aware that people will, in a genuine way, want you to help them, listen to them, or advocate for them.

This can involve little hassles like asking you to introduce them to a good-looking friend, or bigger annoyances like using you to become popular themselves. Don't give in to ridiculous demands and certainly don't let yourself be used. But also don't forget where you came from. Help others make friends and be there for them within reasonable limits.

If you find yourself having any of these problems, don't get too freaked out. Unless it's a dangerous situation like a stalker, you know how to deal with the hassles of popularity. Act according to the principles you've learned in this book.

Handle each problem with detachment, charm, flexibility, and especially assertiveness. Make your responses ethical and within your moral boundaries too. And, for goodness sakes, avoid creating or fanning the flames of drama.

If you've never had a lot of friends and wannabe friends, you've probably never had to tell anyone "no." Now's a good time to remember what you learned in Chapter 27, and master saying "no" in a firm, but friendly, manner.

If you say "no" in an assertive way while remaining cool, most people will stop pestering you, but you won't have ticked anyone off. On the other hand, if you can't say "no" without being rude and aggressive, you will get the person in question to leave you alone, probably permanently, along with others who'll want nothing to do with you.

There isn't any homework from this section because the "rock star problem" is probably not something you've encountered yet. Just keep it in the back of your mind and be ready to deal with it in a mature fashion if it comes. Because trust me, if you become popular, it will arrive at some point. However, in most situations, the "problem" of being popular isn't a bad one to have.

CHAPTER 30

THEORY OF GRAVITY

A few years ago, I took my twin brother David to a football game at the school where I used to teach. As we were walking in the gate, several of my students rushed up to greet us and started talking to us. They were very excited to see me at an afterschool event. After talking to these kids for a while, several others who were walking by also joined in, wanting to talk to my brother and me. Once a few minutes had passed, about fifteen kids were standing around us, all wanting to share in the social experience.

That day David and I encountered "Celebrity Gravity," which is what happens when you become popular: you have a way of drawing others closer to you. And it works exponentially. The more people become interested in you, the greater the chance that even more new people will want to join in, doubling, even tripling, the original number of individuals hoping to be around you.

This is illustrated by a psychological phenomenon, which is covered in the book Influence by Robert Cialdini. Basically, if other people are doing something, the rest of us are more likely to join in (10). If you see five hundred students running in the opposite direction of your school, you're pretty likely to join in the stampede, and assume they know something you don't. This principle is also why product endorsements are so successful. When someone, whether a celebrity or an average person, tells us he or she likes a product, it makes us feel comfortable in our choices. It's basically an acceptable form of peer pressure. Another term for this is "social proof."

In the realm of people and relationships, this social proof works much the same way. People see you surrounded by others and they can make several assumptions about you. First, they know that you are safe and approachable. You're not going to kill or harm them because others have talked to you and survived (yes, this is really why it works at a basic "brain" level). Second, it proves you are worth knowing. If you are holding the attention of five people, then you must be at least slightly interesting.

And, if you are holding the attention of a thousand people, you must be extremely interesting. Celebrities are social proof in action: they hold the attention of hundreds of thousands of individuals, maybe even millions. That's why movies, albums, and even some products brag about the numbers they've sold on labels or advertisements.

This concept was shown through an experiment several years ago, which Cialdini references in his book. Scientists asked a person to stand on a busy city street and look at the sky. The vast majority of people simply walked past. However, when researchers asked *several* people to look up at the sky, a large number of bystanders stopped and also looked at the sky. They assumed that one lone weirdo wasn't worth their effort. But, if a crowd thought it was important to look up, then those walking by thought they had better look up as well. This is an important lesson for anyone wanting to become popular. After all, as I've mentioned before, popularity is just a numbers game.

There are several ways to use social proof to your advantage. First, if you are a high-value person, then this celebrity gravity will happen naturally. A smart, witty, outgoing, and good-looking person who shares those traits with the world will attract others to his or her side. You just have to get out, approach others, and let the gravity happen naturally. Believe me, it works with no more effort than just being your normal and excellent self.

If you have trouble getting a crowd to form around you, then remember that most people just want to enjoy life. The vast majority of children, teens, and even adults aren't really thrilled about life. Most of them hate school or their jobs, don't get along all that well with their families, and have lots of stress from a variety of sources. They would love to enter into an enjoyable reality, but they can't seem to find it on a regular basis. If you can provide an escape for them by making them laugh, giving them positive attention, and meeting their emotional needs, then they will come to you.

This is exactly what happened to David and me at the football game. Anyone can tell you that a teacher or principal who makes you feel good about yourself and actually meets your emotional needs is pretty rare. I did that as a teacher, at least for the vast majority of my students, so they all wanted to see me and talk to me when they saw me outside of the classroom.

The sun's gravity attracts the earth; you will attract all kinds of people to you.

And, when those students gathered around us, even those teens who didn't know me personally still wanted to come over and see what all the fuss was about. That I had a twin brother made me (and him) even more interesting. If you go out and give the world laughter, joy, and fun (and something a little unique, like our twin status), you too will have gravity wherever you go.

Your homework for this chapter is to engage in some people-watching. Go out to a crowded place and play a little game: find the popular person. It's usually not hard. Look for the man or woman who has a bunch of people around him or her. Watch the interaction among everyone involved. Also, notice how even strangers seem to be attracted to the action, even if it's just by smiling when they walk past. Write down what you observed and think about how you can use what you've seen in your own life to attract more friends.

Then, I want you to do the same thing at your school. Don't make it too obvious that you're staring at people (it's creepy), but notice how the "popular" kids look and act, and how others respond to them. At a school, you should definitely see the gravity that comes with popularity. You can even see it with some of your teachers. If an assignment is really hard, students will swarm the teacher's desk. At that point, even if she's a jerk, she'll be quite popular because she has what people want; in this case, it's the answers.

Chapter 31

Be Contagious

Back in the-mid 1990's my family and I went to downtown Columbus, Ohio for Fourth of July fireworks. We spent the night at a fancy hotel. While we were taking the elevator up to our room, the sound of screeching females pierced my ears. Three preteen girls in the elevator with me were screaming uncontrollably. I looked over and discovered why. Alfonso Ribeiro, who played "Carlton" on the popular television show *The Fresh Prince of Bel Air*, was in the elevator.

I was too scared to ask for his autograph in the elevator, but just being in the same space as him was extremely exciting. When I went back to my room, I spent the next couple of hours planning ways to find him again and get my picture taken with him. I wasn't obsessed. Heck, I didn't even really like the show all that much. But, I was definitely excited. The possibility of seeing him and being associated with him, for some reason, had created a spark within me.

Think about your favorite celebrity or even someone very popular at your school right now. What kinds of feelings come to mind? Excitement? Nervousness? Now imagine actually being with that person and becoming a part of his or her inner circle? Even more excited? Even more nervous? If the answer is "yes" to all these questions, then don't feel weird. You're normal. Famous, popular, and high-value people create a contagious excitement. Just by being themselves, they get others excited about life.

If you've taken a psychology class, you may have heard the name of Abraham Maslow. He studied the concept of "peak experiences," which are intense moments of excitement, joy, wonder and awe that humans experience. For most of us, these peak experiences define our lives in ways that normal experiences do not. This is why people vividly recall meeting a famous celebrity or remember details about a personal tragedy, even though both may have happened years ago, but can't tell you what they had for lunch earlier in the week.

Peak experiences, by their very name, mean that they are some of the top moments of our lives. We value them because they are so rare. This explains why meeting famous people, coming of age rituals like a "sweet sixteen" birthday, great vacations, and amazing concerts are so memorable and meaningful. However, there's no rule that we can't have peak moments more frequently.

Your goal in becoming popular is to create little peak moments everywhere you go. Unless you are a famous celebrity, meeting you probably isn't going to be a life-changing event for other people. However, being around you should be a day-changing event at the very least. Your goal should be to make life more exciting and more interesting for everyone you meet. If others know that being around you will make their day more special, they will want to spend time with you.

Another interesting aspect of peak experiences is that they can change people's outlook, even if temporarily. This happened when I met Alfonso Ribeiro in the elevator at the Hyatt Hotel. As I look back, I don't remember anything else about the day, except my encounter with him. Even if I was in a bad mood or low energy, meeting him changed me. It made me excited, happy, and gave me a new focus: finding a way to get a photo with him. You want people to feel the same way when they meet you.

You may think it sounds like a difficult task, but it's not. It's simply about being happy and excited about life. Once you achieve that goal, then you have to go out and share that excitement with the world. Believe me, it's extremely contagious. Go into a stuffy place and start smiling. People may think you're weird at first, but eventually others will start smiling too. Everyone wants to feel good and if you give them the opportunity to laugh, feel a little joy, and have someone to look up to, they'll love you. It's what being popular is all about.

However, some days you may not be the most exciting and upbeat person. To create contagious excitement, you may have to pump yourself up when you go to school or go out for the weekend. Some people find listening to music or watching uplifting clips from YouTube helpful. Others pump themselves up through exciting self-talk, like by telling themselves how awesome they are. Pick whatever works.

Personally, I don't even need any special techniques anymore. I get excited enough just by the thought of being me and sharing myself with the world. You may think I'm cocky, but once you become popular, you'll know exactly what I'm talking about.

Once you become joyful, happy, and excited, you must go out and interact positively with everyone you encounter, from the bus driver on the way to school, to the nerd in your math class. Sure, you'll run into angry individuals who may blow you off or make fun of you, but the vast majority of people will appreciate your attitude and friendliness. In most cases, they will want to join in. And, don't worry if you're not interacting with so-called popular kids. You become popular one person at a time, even if in the beginning that only applies to the smelly bus driver and the nerd sitting by himself at lunch.

I want to give a small warning before you go out and accidentally pester the world. You don't want to be a "Buddy the Elf after he ingests maple syrup" type of person (see the Christmas movie *Elf* if this reference is lost on you). Don't be so peppy and optimistic (and fake) that others want to punch you in the face rather than interact with you. Be energetic, fun, and exciting in a way that fits with your personality too.

Your assignment for this chapter is to record a "morning blitz" of affirmations. The easiest way is to use your cell phone or tablet. Write down a few short affirmations like "You are excited, happy, and ready for a great day." Then, record your script on your cell phone or another recorder. Play it first thing every morning, as soon as you awake. Maybe even make it the tone for your cell phone alarm.

I've been doing this for a while and even on days where I may feel a little tired initially, hearing my morning blitz gets me in the right state to go out and act like the popular person I know I am: excited about life and spreading that excitement to others. And, by the way, my brother and I did end up getting a picture with Ribeiro, making our friends very jealous.

CHAPTER 32

YOU CAN'T GO BACK (IN TIME)

When I first started writing this book, the area where I live experienced a rare mini-tornado. It was a scary moment for my family and me, especially after watching one of the giant trees in our yard snap like a twig from the "safety" of our shaking house. Thankfully, my home wasn't damaged, but I had to clean up nearly an acre of downed limbs, branches, and yard objects that had blown from my yard across my neighbors' lawns and all the way onto the adjoining golf course.

I was busy clearing trees and cutting limbs when a man pulled into my driveway and offered to saw up everything in my yard for a couple hundred dollars. At first, I thought I would do the job myself. After all, I was raised to be independent and tough-minded. A little tornado wasn't about to stop me! However, I thought about his offer for a second and ended up paying him the money. I wasn't being lazy, although he saved me hours of work. The incident reminded me of an important popularity axiom: you can't go back (in time).

This phrase means that no matter how hard we may try or want to, we can't return to the past and re-do our lives. That embarrassing moment in first grade, the flubbed first kiss with the crush, and all those other horror-inducing moments are stuck in the past of reality. We can get over the past, learn from it, and maybe, if we're really mindful, even forget about it. But, we can't change it.

Reading MJ DeMarco's Millionaire Fastlane completely changed my outlook on life. He notes that rich and popular people are generous with their money, but stingy with their time. Poor people are usually generous with their time, but not their money. What he means is that people who give hours each day to menial jobs, watching sports, and playing video games will almost always end up poor. On the other hand, those individuals who use their time executing great ideas and promoting themselves will end up very rich (and famous).

It makes sense if you think about it. Your most valuable asset is your time. Money is pretty much unlimited with a government printing press, while you are limited in time to twenty four hours a day, seven days a week, 365 days a year. And, even if you're extremely lucky, you'll likely get one hundred of those years. You can't change time no matter how much you whine, complain, or beg your Maker. And, since that time is scarce, it is extremely valuable. Or it should be.

However, look at how most people treat their time. A lot of adults give sixty hours a week to a job they hate so they can buy a slightly nicer car to impress their equally miserable neighbors. Some of them even spend hours a day building up virtual farms on Facebook or being wizards in alternate universes. And they accuse teens of being immature! But, you don't get off the hook so easily.

Many teenagers I talk to text mindlessly or engage in pointless drama and debates without even realizing it. That doesn't even include the teens I know who are literally addicted to video games and game apps. Given the limitations and value of time, it's amazing how many people spend their lives completely wasting it.

Successful people know the truth about time: it's your greatest asset. If you use your time to come up with great ideas, network with others, build your brand, or pursue your goals, you'll achieve the freedom and success that your friend who plays Xbox all day or your neighbor who sends ten thousand text messages each month could only dream of.

Consequently, a popular person must always place the highest value on his or her time. Being famous and loved by a variety of people requires you to meet and influence as many people as possible. However, you can't, even if you wish, add hours to the day. It'd be nice to have thirty hours a day to promote yourself and build up your number of friends (or meet that special someone) while everyone else has twenty-four, but it isn't happening.

However, you can do what most people don't: maximize their time. I picked on gamers, obsessive texters, and those indentured to their jobs (for the record, I play video games sometimes, love to text, and work a lot of hours), but even if that isn't you, don't think you're getting off easy.

The average American watches over four hours of television a day (11). When you add surfing the net and other mindless activities, it probably pushes the total time staring at a screen to seven or eight hours. With six hours of school, extracurricular activities, and a job, added to eight hours of sleep, that doesn't leave many productive minutes for teens to make themselves more popular. And, I'm sure the weekends aren't any better when sporting events, hanging with friends and family, and sleeping in are given high priority.

Another point DeMarco makes in his book that relates to time is how all successful people understand that their success comes from a process, not an event. In other words, behind every popular person is a process of hard work that led to his or her current state. And, being popular requires lots of time. For example, before they were famous, most successful musicians, actors, and athletes experienced "lean" times when they worked extremely hard for little reward. Then, somewhere down the line, their efforts paid off handsomely. Make sure your time is spent becoming successful and popular and isn't wasted on activities you'll look back on later and regret doing (see Chapter 33).

So, I want you to start jealously guarding your time right now. Get out a sheet of paper (yes, this is your assignment) and map out your typical day for both Monday through Friday and the weekend. Be honest about what you actually do. If you crush virtual candy all day, I promise I won't laugh (too hard). Now, go through your schedule and find ways you can cut down on wasting time and start bettering yourself and making friends.

Trim your video game playing time to an hour a week. Stop sleeping nine hours a night. Quit mindlessly texting. Turn off the TV. Disable your phone's data (unless you're sending a snap to someone cute). Get busy on something positive like meeting people and cultivating a talent. Or maybe just spend time with family and friends, and gradually work to expand that circle. That beats watching a bunch of reality show "stars" anyway. Regardless, make the most of your time because it's an aspect of life you absolutely can't control.

You see, I wasn't just being snobby or extravagant by paying some guy to cut up my fallen trees. I used the three hours I saved that afternoon to work on my business. I wrote content for my websites and worked on other writing projects (including this book). I paid a couple hundred bucks to buy the time to make even more money and influence even more people. If you truly want to become popular, then you want to make sure your time is spent becoming the person you truly want to be. The next chapter will help you achieve this.

CHAPTER 33

TAKE A RISK

In college, I had a good friend who was a senior when I was a freshman. We hung out a lot at a certain establishment that was also frequented by a beautiful young lady. I knew that my friend had a big crush on her. And I don't blame him. She was pretty, smart, and friendly. As graduation approached, he told me how he needed to sit down with her and tell her his feelings before he left town. I got nervous just thinking about *him* doing it. My advice was to forget about it. He ignored me and, about two weeks before graduation, pulled her aside and laid out his feelings.

There has been some scientific research on the topic of regrets. One study showed that while humans tend to regret both actions they've done and failed to do, the most long-lasting regret tends to focus on missed opportunities (12). In other words, the most emotionally

JONATHAN AND DAVID BENNETT

damaging form of regret is when we failed to take advantage of (or create) an opportunity that is no longer possible. Since another study notes adults spend on average forty-five minutes a week dwelling on their regrets (13), failing to act in certain situations can leave a person with a lifelong emotional toll. Teens have regret too, but the longer a person lives, the more likely regret will rear its ugly head.

When we want to act in some way, but fail to do so, it usually comes down to one word (in spite of various excuses): fear. In some cases that feeling of fear can be a legitimate and good thing. For example, if we think about jumping over Niagara Falls, fear of death or serious harm will likely stop us from such a bone-headed act. Also, fear of our parents, the police, or bad health effects may keep someone from trying drugs. This is also a good thing. However, in many cases, our desire to act is stopped by an irrational fear called "anxiety." Irrational anxiety is never a good thing and is one of the biggest contributors to regret. Sometimes we "play it safe" simply because we fear taking a good risk that could have incredible rewards.

My recommendation, if you want to become popular, and, I might add, successful, is to take reasonable, educated, and safe (RES) risks and do so frequently. I am a naturally cautious person, which has served me well in some ways. I've never tried drugs and I have no credit card debt, for example. Yet, I still live with a lot of "what if?" type of regrets. I realize that while being cautious with chemicals and not taking on debt are good traits, being cautious with other aspects of life (like self-promotion) is not. Consequently, one of my declarations (see Chapter 2) is to take at least one reasonable, educated, and safe risk every single day. And, I follow through on it. I've still avoided doing stupid things, but my life is more adventurous and abundant. Hold on, though. Before you go out and do something dumb that will get you in trouble, finish reading this chapter!

First, I want to define the kind of risk that I think you should take. I'm talking about a "good" risk, one that has a lot of upside that doesn't put you or other people in serious danger. This risk, once again, is reasonable, educated, and safe (RES). Many risks that teenagers take on a regular basis (speeding, drugs, unprotected sex, etc.) are "bad risks." They have very little upside and put the person taking them and others in danger. They are irrational, show little foresight, and are unsafe. For clarity, I'm going to examine each aspect of a good risk in some detail.

The first aspect of a good risk is that it is reasonable (R). This means that you've thought about the risk and weighed the pros and cons (see next paragraph). The reward should always be worth the risk. For example, investing one thousand dollars in a very risky stock to possibly earn eleven hundred dollars isn't a good enough reward to possibly lose the original thousand. Part of being reasonable is that the outcome also has to be possible for you to achieve. Making the high school football team when you're a little out of shape is possible. If you show up at the New York Jets training camp grossly obese and with no football experience, you have to know that making the team would be impossible. So, it's irrational.

The second aspect of a good risk is that it is educated (E). This means that you've researched the upside (reward) and the downside of the risk. Then, you can make an informed decision about whether to take the risk. Maybe a doctor wanted to put you on medication that you or your parents thought would help you with a mental issue. It's certainly a risk, possibly a good one, but it's still important to research and know the facts about the drug. Sometimes researching the facts can be tough because you have to make a decision quickly (like whether or not to ask a pretty girl to dance). In this case, you may have to go with your gut instinct or what you've learned in the past.

If a risk is dumb, like taking drugs, then stop, and don't do it.

Finally, a good risk must always be safe (S). I don't mean that a risk is easy or comfortable. It's not going to be either or it wouldn't, by definition, be a risk. By safe, I mean it's not going to cause harm (physical or otherwise) to you or someone else. This is perhaps the most important part of a "good' risk. Most people will recover from stupid and irrational risks. However, there are many teenagers who die, go to jail, or develop a host of other problems based on a stupid and unsafe decision.

I also want to note that you can't let anxiety masquerade as any of these legitimate concerns. For example, anxiety can tell you asking a girl out is irrational. Anxiety can tell you that all the evidence a girl likes you is false. Anxiety can also tell you that asking her out will kill you (emotionally, at least). Anxiety sucks! So, don't let it cloud your thinking when deciding to take risks.

If anxiety threatens to hamper your success, talk yourself through the three parts of a good risk (not out loud if you're in public). Let's use the above example to show why anxiety is a nuisance when it tries to stop a guy from asking out a pretty girl. Asking out a girl, if he is attracted to girls, is very reasonable. It's normal and expected. And, if he's even somewhat attractive, she will likely seriously consider giving him a date. Also, while "approach anxiety" may make him feel like he's going to die, unless she is somehow dangerous, like wielding a gun or escorted by her NFL-player dad, he's in no real danger. See how feelings of anxiety could mislead our young man in the example? Don't let your anxiety stop you from taking good risks.

I'm going to give a few examples of good and bad risks and break them down by categories:

Good risk - A healthy person trying out for the football team.

- Rational: Absolutely.

- Educated: Sure, as long as it's for a respectable league that upholds safety guidelines.

- Safe: While playing sports always carries injury risks, the vast majority of high school athletes are not harmed by them.

Good risk - Auditioning for a part in a local play.

- Rational: Yes.

- Educated: Check to make sure there is a need for your talents.

- Safe: Of course.

Bad risk - Trying illegal drugs.

- Rational: Not really.

- Educated: No, since millions in the USA are hooked on drugs.

- Safe: Considering the addiction and overdose potential, no.

Bad risk - Excessively speeding.

- Rational: Maybe, if you are late.

- Educated: Not really, since teens and speed lead to many accidents every year; states generally have harsher penalties for teen drivers who violate traffic laws.

- Safe: No. Can lead to death or serious injury to self or others.

Hopefully, you can see what constitutes a good risk and a bad risk. Notice how the good risks are all difficult, perhaps anxiety-inducing tasks, but also have the reward of making you popular. Also, notice how the bad risks may give you short-term benefits (for example, taking drugs may temporarily numb emotional pain or help you fit in), but have serious downsides, both short-term (like an overdose) and long-term (a life of addiction).

In my second career at a substance abuse counseling agency, I see the results of bad choices every day: addiction, STD's, criminal records, overdose deaths, etc. Bad risks can have serious consequences and really can ruin lives (or end them prematurely). However, good risks (like starting a business) can also have great rewards. Just make sure your risks are rational, educated, and safe (RES) and you will find they usually pay off. And, if they don't, they won't leave you worse off than when you started.

I hate poison ivy and my fear of this plant took an irrational hold over me in the past. Consequently, I didn't enjoy the outdoors for years. One day, however, I decided that I really wanted to hike a new trail with a couple of friends. As I started the hike, I saw poison ivy along the beginning of the path, which normally would've deterred me. I told myself that I could step over or walk around anything that looked like poison ivy rather than irrationally refusing to go anywhere within one hundred feet of the plant. I put one foot in front of the other and actually went on the hike! I saw beautiful areas of the park I'd never visited before and it was a challenging workout. I now hike that trail regularly in the summer. It was a risk, but a good one, and the reward ended up being worth the effort.

So, what about my friend who confessed his love to his crush? She didn't have those same feelings for him. However, by sharing his feelings, they developed a deeper friendship and grew closer, even if not in the way he expected. In addition, he didn't have to live with the regret of knowing that he never tried to have a romantic relationship with her. He may have failed, but at least he tried. That's more than the other ninety-nine percent of people who don't act, and have to live with long-term regret for the rest of their lives.

Your homework for this chapter is to write out four "good" risks you can take over the next four days. Write out the risk, then fill in the details for each category (rational, educated, and safe). If you determine that it's rational, educated, safe and beneficial for your quest for popularity, then go out and do it. And, don't let anxiety stop you. You also may consider adding "take a good risk each day" to your declarations (see Chapter 2).

CHAPTER 34

THE BODY TELLS A LOT

When I was a teacher, I had a meeting with my former principal that I'll never forget. I was presenting a new idea for student learning to my fellow teachers. All my colleagues looked relaxed and open, but my boss had her arms crossed, was leaning back, and was frowning. She had the final say, and my idea died right there.

But, it wasn't exactly a surprise. I knew, just from a quick glance at their body language, that my colleagues were at least open to my thoughts. I also knew that my boss would never give my idea a chance. And this was before any of them even said a word. Your body communicates just as much, if not more, about your intentions than the words you use.

If you want to become popular, you can say and do all the right things, but still have your best efforts sabotaged by an unlikely, subconscious source: your body. If your body language is closed, all your charming words and witty routines will backfire. The people you're trying to win over will subconsciously notice the lack of congruity between your allegedly open words and your obviously closed body language. If you want others to feel comfortable and open around you, your body has to convey comfort and openness too.

Body language is a complicated subject, but fortunately it can be simplified to a few basic principles. Generally speaking, if your body is closed, you are viewed as closed; if it is open, you're seen as open. Thus, gestures like crossed legs, crossed arms, covering your neck, etc. are seen as walls to interaction. On the other hand, being spread out, having open arms, open thighs, and open lips (a smile) show others you are welcoming to interaction. Another basic principle is that people point toward or face the direction of people they like, and away from those they don't (14).

As far as confidence goes, keeping your head high and walking with your chest out slightly are great confident gestures, especially for men. Look at the way Superman is drawn. He's clearly confident. Another great way to show confidence is to make consistent eye contact. Don't stare excessively, but you should leave every conversation consciously knowing the eye color of the other person.

You may be a little skeptical, but keep in mind that these body language cues are typically made and received subconsciously. So, you may be projecting that you're closed and the person you're with will be picking it up too, but neither of you will even be aware of it. Practice being open and confident, even using a mirror if necessary.

In fact, if you are having trouble with body language, simply watch your teachers and fellow students. Likely you can tell when your teacher is annoyed with you before she says a word. Also, if your girlfriend moves away when you try to put your arm around her, then you don't have to be told that something is bothering her, and that "something" is likely you!

When interacting with others, pay special attention to your body language. This is because in many cases, the body language of being closed is identical to the body language of nervousness. So, a person's body language can scream annoyed, closed, and snobby, when in reality, he or she is simply shy or awkward. When in situations that make you anxious, you must be even more aware of what your body is saying to those around you.

There are some special rules that govern body language for romantic relationships. Although this book isn't concerned only with getting you dates, a popular person will almost always get romantic attention from other people. So, it's important to know the body language "signs of attraction."

I know many female readers may not believe it, but it's actually not too difficult to tell if a guy is romantically attracted to you. You just have to remember that there are different types of guys. In general, an outgoing male will approach you and start talking to you to show that he likes you. A shy or awkward guy will often stare at you from across the room for long periods of time. It's usually that simple. Guys, in their body language, are typically fairly direct about their intentions, even if the shy ones can't quite muster up the courage to follow through with the intentions they've shown.

It's a little harder, if you're a guy, to tell if a girl likes you romantically. Females are often more subtle, and many men are socially dense or second-guess themselves. Below, I've listed the most common ways a girl shows a guy she's interested. Of course, there are many more. Female readers may want to practice some of these body language cues to show the guys you like that you're attracted to them.

Here are the signs of attraction a girl will often give to a guy (and girls often don't know they're doing it):

- Playing with her hair, twisting it, etc.

- Showing her exposed neck or wrist.

- Her feet and/or belly-button are pointed toward the guy she likes.

- She tells him her name before he asks.

- Genuine laughter.

- Picking lint off of his shirt, putting his exposed tag back in shirt, etc.

- Repeatedly touching him in a conversation.

- Smiling.

- Giving him the "once over," i.e. looking up and down his body, "checking him out."

- Sustained and penetrating eye contact.

Obviously, my discussion on body language is far from complete. In fact, the topic of body language is an extremely fascinating one that would be to your benefit to master. If you have the time, I would highly recommend that you check out some more advanced books on the subject. See the Recommended Reading section at the end of the book. However, the basic rules outlined here will get you started.

Your homework for this chapter is to go out and observe body language. Go to a coffee shop, mall, party, or even a class. You're there to people watch (although don't make it obvious). Observe how their bodies tell you what people are thinking. Can you find people who are happy? What about mad, sad, or bored? Who is closed to interaction and who looks fun? Who is romantically attracted to whom? Which people obviously can't stand each other? Write down your observations.

It shouldn't be too hard to figure out what each person is thinking. We are pretty darn good at reading body language naturally. The problems arise when we second-guess ourselves. If you're looking for that special someone, keep an eye out for signs of attraction. And I want you to find an open person and approach. Just go up and say "hello." See what happens. It's preparation for the next chapter.

The next few pages contain images and some analysis. Look at them before you go out and try it on real people.

The guy here is confident and happy, and is standing straight up, with his chest out and head up. He likes her, but is barely showing it. The girl is enjoying his company. She is playing with her hair, showing her wrist, smiling, and pointing her naval towards him.

What happened?? He did something to creep her out, because she is physically moving away from him, her feet are pointed away, and her naval area is pointed away. He seems clueless, but she has lost interest for sure.

Both people are "body blocking," which means they are uncomfortable, or not liking something about the other. This indicates they are closed to each other. If you are this guy, now is probably not the time to ask her out.

What is she projecting? Her legs and arms are crossed. She is also "hiding"

behind the table and drink. She is telegraphing "stay away." If she wanted to meet

new people, she should open up. Guys: approach with caution!

The next three chapters explain the three-part process of meeting new people (the approach, building of rapport, and the close). Right now, you should have the "theory" of being more popular mastered, as well as having gained some real-world practice. Now you're moving from practice to the game itself.

CHAPTER 35

POPULAR TEENS KNOW HOW TO APPROACH

When I was sixteen, I went to a birthday party of a guy I barely knew. A friend dragged me along. I saw a cute girl across the room, and after over an hour of building up the courage, finally decided to walk over and introduce myself. At that exact moment, another guy approached her and they started talking. Was it horrible timing? Perhaps, except I had a window of over an hour that I wasted. I blew it because I had a common problem that plagues males and females of all ages: I was scared to death of approaching people.

Overcoming the fear of talking to new people is one the biggest advantages that will help you become popular and increase your number of friends. Obviously, if you're too afraid to meet others, they can't be your friends. So, for this chapter, I'm primarily going to focus on overcoming that fear. Once you get the courage to approach others, you can use the other skills you've learned in the book, like humor, to start and continue the actual conversation.

The study of evolutionary psychology shows us that the brains of males and females evolved differently throughout human history, so the sexes are wired to interact with each other in different ways. This is why I've included a separate section below for both males and females. I highly recommend every reader master the information in this entire chapter, in order to understand the role of the opposite sex in the approach.

For guys:

If you're a guy and want to be popular, either with other guys or with girls, you have to keep a couple of things in mind. First, the male social order is hierarchical at its core. You have leaders and followers. There are some people who fall in the middle, but for the most part you're either one or the other. You can probably see this at your school. The most popular guys are likely the ones who take the lead in some way, like sports or even as bullies. Even in groups of people not connected to sports, like the gamers or the musicians, there are usually leaders and followers.

In ancient times, being a leader was usually the result of a man's physical (and mental) strength. The "alpha male" was normally the toughest guy in a tribe. He could fight off competing tribes, outsmart the competition, and hunt dangerous game. If someone else decided he wanted to run the tribe, that guy would have to be stronger than the current chief. He'd have to fight the reigning leader and likely one of them would die or be severely injured. Similar power struggles also occur in the colonies of other primates (like apes and chimpanzees).

It wasn't any easier for a guy who wanted to find a mate. If he approached a woman, he'd have to make sure she wasn't "taken" in some way by the tribe's alpha male and his inner circle. If she was? Possible death or a serious beating. Consequently, the male brain has wired over time to have a healthy fear of approaching others, especially strange women and fellow males in positions of power. No joke.

You're probably wondering why I'm sharing all of this. Well, fast-forward to the twenty-first century. We're not fighting wooly mammoths and our leaders are more likely to be businessmen and community pillars than brawny linebacker types. Still, our brains haven't caught up to the current reality. Male brains still have a strong fear of approaching strangers, like my story at the start of the chapter illustrates. While some of this is justified (the guy on the corner with the bulging biceps and look of murder in his eye), a lot of it is not (the sweet and pretty girl I saw at the party). This primal fear is often called "approach anxiety," and every guy will experience some degree of it in his life.

Don't believe me? Think of the hottest girl in your high school. Now envision yourself approaching her and trying to get her number. Feeling nauseated? Now remember what I said earlier in this chapter, about the followers and the leaders? Well, you need to turn into a leader. And, that involves approaching new people and interacting with them. Sorry if this is making you even more nauseated! Just remember, that while approach anxiety is hard-wired into the male brain, it can be controlled. Outgoing and popular guys, like the one who beat me to the punch when I was sixteen, do it all the time. For the most part, overcoming approach anxiety involves taking control of your brain. It is yours, after all. The tips below should help ease your fear of approaching others.

The first way to combat approach anxiety is to remember that approaching someone won't kill you. You're not going to undo hundreds of thousands of years of evolution in a week, but the rational side of your brain can keep the rest of it in check. Each time you are ready to approach a man or woman, take charge of your brain. Acknowledge that your brain (at least the subconscious part) is trying to sabotage you, and then remind your brain that you will survive. There is no death by rejection. Take note that this advice applies in normal and safe situations. If you are in an unsafe or unfamiliar situation, then always listen to your gut instinct and use common sense. Remember the guy with the biceps and look of murder? Yeah, don't approach that guy or his girlfriend.

Second, approach anxiety can be countered by mastering the other techniques in this book like detachment, flexibility, humor, open body language, etc. The more confident, high-value, and detached you become, the less approach anxiety will rule your life. Basically, as you become more popular, it gets easier. Do you think celebrities like

Kanye West have a lot of approach anxiety? I highly doubt it.

Finally, the key to destroying approach anxiety is to approach others often. The more you do it, the more your brain will realize that approaching new people won't kill you. It will even discover that meeting strangers can actually be pretty fun. In fact, meeting strangers *is* extremely fun, so be sure to pay attention to this chapter's advice. After all, approaching others leads to some pretty awesome outcomes like getting attention, befriending new people, and developing romantic relationships. That's a pretty good deal, even if part of your brain initially doesn't want you to do it.

For women:

Girls typically interact with people in different ways than their male counterparts. While the female structure is still hierarchical, it's often more subtle and complex. Many of you know that high school relationships among girls often thrive on drama. However, being truly popular, at any age, typically means rising above this drama and forming more meaningful relationships.

When trying to befriend other girls, it's important to let them know you're not a threat to them or their interests. A lot of girls have their guard up because they are so used to dysfunctional friendships. If you're approaching a new group of girls, find common ground, use humor, and be genuine. Don't act like you're going to break up their established group or like you're trying to conceal the fact that you're

JONATHAN AND DAVID BENNETT

trying to break up the established group.

If you are just scared to death of making new friends or overly shy, read the section for the guys on approach anxiety. Although the male brain is slightly different from the female one, the approach anxiety tips are useful to both sexes.

When it comes to meeting guys, I have some good news for ladies. The job of approaching and asking you out belongs to the males. However, the girl still has an important job: being open to that interaction and letting the guy know that fact. Remember the chapter on body language (Chapter 34)? If you're around a guy you like, use some of the techniques that you learned there to be more open to interaction. However, some guys are really dense and shy. So, if a guy seems like he's attracted to you and is too shy to approach and talk to you, you can always go over and talk to him. It's not 1955. Just do it.

For everyone:

In the end, the best advice for both sexes to meet new people is to relax and have a good time. Remember, approaching others or talking to those who approach you isn't going to kill you. In fact, think about all of the amazing people out there whom you'd love to meet. If you don't approach them and they don't approach you, then you'll never connect with them.

The risk of approach seems like it's a big one, since rejection can be hard to take. However, in reality, being rejected by a total stranger you'll likely never see again is a pretty small risk. But, if you meet a new best friend, get a boyfriend or girlfriend, or widen your circle of friends considerably, then an approach could be one of the best things you've ever done. You can approach other people knowing that the risk is minimal, yet the potential reward could be life-changing.

I also want to give a few tips about approaches. First, always approach safe people who will share your values. There are plenty of good people out there. Don't waste your time on losers. Second, although I talk about "random" approaches, remember that nothing is ever truly random. Where you decide to approach is important because it tells a lot about you and the people you're meeting.

So, approach others in places where you're comfortable and at your best. If you love music, it could be a concert. If you're a natural athlete, then meet new people at games and events. One of my biggest mistakes in college was trying to meet people at places where I wasn't truly comfortable. Be your best self and hang out in spots where that best self can shine. Finally, use the various techniques you've learned in this book to make the approach unique and worthwhile for the person you're planning to meet. You don't want to be perceived as boring and low-value to a person you worked so hard to get up the nerve to meet.

Your homework is to go out tonight and approach five random people. However, let me give you a word of advice: it's best to go somewhere you can be comfortable and where people are anticipating an approach, at least if this is your first time. I'd recommend a social event, a friend's party, or a busy coffee shop or mall. Remember to use your humor routines. Try to keep the conversation going, but at this point don't stress too much about follow-up. Just approach five people and talk to them. If you want, you can ask for their number or social media contact information, but you don't have to. Then, write down your observations.

CHAPTER 36

IF YOU BUILD IT, THEY WILL COME

A few years ago, my friends and I went out to a restaurant to celebrate the Fourth of July. The waitress was obviously not happy to be working on a holiday and I couldn't blame her. We used our humor routines and tried other ways to be funny and charming, but everything fell flat. She didn't need to be entertained that night. What she needed was someone who would listen to her. We were flexible, so we shifted gears and just listened for a while. What she wanted, and even needed, was someone to simply hear her out. We did a little thing called "rapport building."

Rapport comes from a French word that means "to carry back." When you build rapport with someone, you are sending out your words and actions and the other person is sending theirs back, meaning that you both are relating to each other. So, after our little

French lesson, all you really need to know is that building rapport is about developing a relationship with another person.

While the approach may be the most difficult to get started due to approach anxiety, two strangers can usually get along well enough in the beginning. Making small talk about similar situations ("Wow, sure looks like a storm today") and throwing out a few jokes for several minutes is pretty easy. Building rapport, which involves listening and paying attention, is actually a little harder. However, if you took the advice on mindfulness and paying attention to heart (Chapters 12 and 25), then rapport building isn't going to be that tough.

It may be helpful to think of rapport building as getting on the same wavelength with someone else. Have you ever heard someone say, "I like his vibe?" A vibe is a vibration or wave. If you hear a vibration, it's possible to mimic it with your voice or another instrument. It's why the alto section of your school choir is (or should be) in harmony. Look at rapport building the same way. The person you've approached is a unique individual you want to get to know. Find out his or her "vibe," and get in harmony with it.

Obviously, rapport building is a two way street, but most people are passive and wait for the more outgoing one to befriend them. That means you will have to take the lead and be prepared to do most of the rapport building work if you want genuine popularity. This is especially true if you are a man or you're approaching someone shy. Just remember that the more rapport you build and the more comfortable the person becomes, the more your two "wavelengths" will converge. Even if it's hard at first, like with approaching, the rewards can be great. Not only are you possibly meeting cool new people, but you're actually forming real relationships with them. Besides, as with everything else in this book, I have some helpful advice for you, some of which comes from the field of Neuro-Linguistic Programming.

The first tip you can use is called *behavioral mirroring*. As the name implies, you build rapport by mirroring another person's behavior and actions. You can adjust the pitch of your voice, your position, tone, breathing, speed of talking, posture, movement, etc. to match the other person's. If she puts her arms on the table or crosses her legs, you would do the same. Make sure you're subtle; otherwise it may look weird or appear as if you are mocking the person. Behavioral mirroring is very effective at building rapport on a subconscious level.

Another good tip is to use *symbolic mirroring*. This is taking someone else's symbols and using them yourself. For example, if you're a girl and the guy you have a crush on is a vegetarian, then use symbols and language that would resonate with vegetarians. For example, quit wearing leather, and bring up animal rights and animal consciousness in conversation (research them first!), even if you don't fully agree with his views on the matter.

Another example would be if you want to make friends with a co-worker who likes country music. Figure out the symbols and language of that musical genre and incorporate some of it into your lifestyle and conversations. Instead of talking about your daily urban life on 65th

Street, talk about the annual camping trips your family takes to West Virginia. If it doesn't look too silly or out-of-place, add some tasteful cowboy boots to your wardrobe.

If you want to relate to a teacher using symbolic mirroring, stop like, wow, totally talking like a teen (OMG), and speak a little more like an adult. Instead of bringing up your daily drama in conversations with your teachers, discuss something more relevant to them (such as asking about their family life and hobbies).

Also, remember that rapport building doesn't mean you stop being yourself or lose your identity in the process of getting to know another person. You're just entering into someone else's world by using their language, symbols, etc. You can expand your own worldview without turning into a clone. We do this all the time when we interact with people of other cultures.

Another easy way to build rapport is to simply listen. Obviously, there are many cases where you want to talk a lot, like when you approach people in a busy setting and want to show them your high-value. However, to build rapport, you'll have to stop and actually listen at some point. My story at the beginning of the chapter illustrates this well. We won over our waitress solely by listening. Once we heard her feelings and learned more about her situation, she went from being rude and distant to friendly and chatty.

Finally, you should assume rapport. In other words, act like you've already built rapport with the person you've approached. This belief will affect your own body language and attitude, taking some stress from the situation. After all, you wouldn't have any trouble talking to your friends. Assuming rapport may even "trick" the person you've met into thinking you already know them.

I once got free coffee at Dunkin Donuts by doing this. I went in and said to the guy working, "Hey man, how've you been? Long time no see!" While I did see him working before, I showed a level of friendliness way beyond our actual relationship. He assumed he knew me from somewhere and we started talking. Now he always talks to me like we're great friends and I get discounted coffee. Also, I might add, that we actually *have* become acquaintances, another benefit of assuming rapport.

A helpful tip for building rapport is to pay attention (see Chapter 25). First, by paying attention to the person you're getting to know, you will be able to learn their symbols, language styles, etc. You'll also be a better active listener if you're actually paying attention. In addition, generally taking notice of the world around you and actually learning new things will help with rapport building. For example, I try to read about a variety of topics, even those I only have a marginal interest in. That way, when I meet a diverse group of people, I can talk about their interests in a genuine way. Once, I met a guy into hockey. Even though I don't find that sport interesting at all, I knew enough about it generally to build rapport with him.

While I haven't divided this chapter into male and female sections, I was tempted. I think it's worth saying that when men and women are interacting with each other, building rapport is a little more complicated.

If you are a girl talking to a guy, realize that guys often don't think in emotional terms. Males are hard-wired to focus more on facts, numbers, etc. It's why the engineer and accountant professions are overwhelmingly male. It also explains why women rarely play fantasy football or take an interest in sports statistics. So, when talking to a boy, you may want to build rapport by playing down the emotional aspects of the conversation and focus instead on the facts, details, objective observations, etc.

If you are a guy talking to a girl, realize that females typically focus on emotions surrounding an event. An example would be sports. A girl will go to a football game and enjoy the feeling of being a part of something bigger. She will get into the excitement of the game, but likely won't care what Tom Brady's quarterback rating is. In fact, all she may know about Tom Brady is that she thinks he's hot.

Instead of relying on facts and objective observations, guys should try to speak to girls using the language of emotion. This means framing your conversations in terms of experiences and the emotions they caused you to have. Let me give you an example. You drive to meet a girl for coffee. Rather than talking about the details of the trip, your car's horsepower, and other facts, explain how you experienced the trip. You might say, "I saw the coolest thing on the way over. It was a guy dressed as a chicken walking on the side of the road. It made me laugh." You've explained something you saw, but in a way that focuses on experience (what you actually did) and emotions ("it was cool," "it made me laugh").

However, you'll want to avoid being too emotional. Emotionalism comes across to women as needy and girly. An example of emotionalism from the above story would be saying, "There were so many traffic lights on the way over here, I just wanted to cry!" No real man (of any age) should ever say anything like that.

Of course, these rules for building rapport with males and females are just general guidelines. There will always be guys and girls you meet who deviate from these stereotypes. Remember, whatever the circumstance, you will adapt (Chapter 9).

Your homework for this chapter is to go out and build rapport. I know it sounds weird, but try it with someone you know at first. It's low pressure, you can try the techniques without looking silly or condescending, and you'll probably get to know the person a lot better. You'd be amazed how little real rapport often exists between friends and acquaintances.

After you test your skills with some family members or friends, I want you to go out and try it with total strangers. Build rapport with at least two previously unknown people. Ideally they should be people your own age and ones you'd really like to get to know.

CHAPTER 37

SEAL THE DEAL

I'll never forget the volunteer trip I took to North Carolina in high school to help repair houses for the elderly. My group from Ohio was there with other teenagers from Georgia. In addition to helping the less fortunate, I got to know a really nice girl from Atlanta named Lisa. We hung out a lot while repairing houses and on breaks. I really liked Lisa, but as the trip began to come to an end, I was in trouble. I knew if I ever wanted to connect with her again, I'd have to man-up. I'd have to cut through the stress and anxiety and make "the close." Up to that point, it hadn't been one of my strongest traits.

The approach and rapport building processes are pointless if you don't make the close. It's like getting a menu, deciding on an amazing dish, and then being too afraid to order. It's even worse when it involves people. I've never met a person yet who doesn't have some story of missing out on a friendship or romantic relationship because they couldn't, or wouldn't, get some type of contact information. Some people have carried this regret for years, even decades, as they look back on lost opportunities.

For the purposes of this book, "closing" means getting a girl's/guy's contact information for whatever purpose and/or getting into a formal type of relationship with the person. This includes, from a romantic side, "dating" or being "boyfriend and girlfriend" with another person.

There are a variety of psychological reasons why it's hard to make the close. I think for many people, it comes down to a simple lack of confidence: they fear being rejected. It feels pretty bad when you've gotten to know someone and ask for a phone number or other contact information, only to be shot down after all that effort. I also think that talking to someone on a casual basis requires little personal risk. But, actually opening yourself up for continual connection with another human being can be scary if you've had bad or disappointing relationships in the past.

Whether you fear the close or not, if you don't make it, you'll miss out on many opportunities since "closing" allows you to be more intimately connected with others. Being the class clown or an entertainer of strangers may be fun at times, but you still need those deeper, lasting connections too. Here are my guidelines for successfully making the close.

The first is to simply give someone your contact information. Although it's dorky for a high school student, you could always get a business card. Only do this if you actually have a business or talent (like if you're a teen who is selling or giving away your photography services).

In most cases, you won't have a card, so just say something simple and low-stress like, "I've really enjoyed talking with you; maybe we should try this again sometime," and give them your number. Adding a bit of humor and making yourself look good may be helpful too. This could be, "Since I know you had such a good time talking to me, you'll want my number." Say this with a smile, in a friendly or flirtatious way, or else the person will think you're a jerk.

Giving your new connections your contact information has a small disadvantage, however. You must rely on the other person to follow-up. The ideal is to get that person's contact information so you control how the follow-up is done.

Another pretty easy way to close with someone is through social media. You can bring up social media in the conversation, maybe mentioning you want to take a cool photo for your Instagram followers, and asking for suggestions. If the person responds favorably and you know he or she is on Instagram, you not only have started a conversation, you have an "in" when it's time to close.

When you're done with the conversation, you can say, "You're really cool; let's follow each other on Instagram," "That was a great photo idea you gave me; you should follow me on Instagram so you can see it," or something similar. People are often more comfortable adding contacts on social networks than giving out their number, because those networks typically offer more privacy options. In addition, with smart phones and other technology, you can connect on social media with the people you meet right then and there.

If you want to get someone's number or contact information, I also recommend creating a need for the person you're talking with to contact you. For example, if I meet someone I like and want to get to know better, I'll typically bring up my business. I'm always looking for photographers, graphic designers, or others to read and critique my books. If I meet people who can help me, then I can ask them for their number to follow up with business opportunities.

If people think there is a benefit for them, they will happily give you their number, Twitter information, or anything else really. Of course, if you're cool, the benefit could simply be from knowing you and joining your social circle. But, if you use this technique, don't tease people. Actually follow up with them about the topic at hand (if you promise them you'll help them make a YouTube video, get your camera ready), even if you later try to shift the relationship towards friendship or romance.

There are a few guidelines to remember when making the close. First, remember that you'll have to build some comfort and rapport with the person you're trying to "close" with first. Simply going up to another person, saying a few lines, and asking for a number won't usually work. Second, in social settings involving romance, guys are expected to make the close with women. Except in extreme cases, ladies aren't likely to volunteer their information unless they really, really like the guy. Dudes, it's your job!

Finally, it's also best to keep the close process simple. You should get the number or other contact information before the interaction is over. Going back to ask for it later, having someone else get it for you, looking the person up on Facebook when you get home, or any indirect, late, or complicated methods should be avoided. They make you look timid and insecure. A confident and popular person will have no trouble asking for someone's number and will do it before the conversation is over. *If* you came across as very confident and memorable during your original interaction, looking them up and contacting them later may work (it has worked for me), but don't take that risk.

Also, if you fail to make the close, don't feel bad. It's not always a reflection on the job you did or your value. Maybe the person you talked to had a bad day or was distracted by family problems. Some people are also just naturally private or loners. Having said that, most people are happy to make new connections, especially if they think connecting with you has some benefit for them (even socially).

Also, after you've made the close, don't appear overeager. I see this mistake all the time with teens. They will get a number and text the person before either of them even leaves the event! Wait a day at least to follow-up. If your contact is time sensitive, then at least delay several hours. You want the person you've met to think you're high-value, which means you are busy and have other people and opportunities taking up your time. Plus, making the person you're contacting sweat a little isn't so bad. Let them be desperate for your time, not the other way around.

In the end, I actually made the close with Lisa and we wrote letters to each other for a while. This was as the internet was just becoming popular, so neither of us had email then. Looking back, I'm kind of surprised that I was able to make the close. However, I valued my relationship with her, and in the end, I guess I figured it was worth it.

Your homework is to go out to a busy place with lots of teens looking to socialize with others. You should probably pick a Friday or Saturday night. Try to make sure there are plenty of strangers too. I want you to try all three aspects of meeting someone new: approaching, building rapport, and closing.

Try not to leave without getting a new contact. In fact, bring your friends and make it a game; see who can get the most contacts in a night, but be sure to help each other out too. Approaching in pairs is helpful too, because it shows social proof (i.e. you have friends that like you; see Chapter 30). Remember, giving your number or other information is acceptable, but *getting* someone else's phone number, or connecting on social media, is preferable.

CHAPTER 38

BLESS THE WORLD

To be honest, I wasn't sure where to put this chapter. I almost made it chapter one, but after some thought, I felt it belonged at the end, as a summary of what being truly popular is all about.

If you've been paying attention you may have noticed that I've used the word "bless" throughout the entire book. This is intentional and not an attempt to inject religion into my work.

The word "bless" comes from a Germanic root that means "to make sacred through sacrifice." If you're rolling your eyes right now, bear with me. This actually has a lot to do with being popular.

When you go out in the world and share your wit, humor, openness, and high-value self, you are giving of yourself. You are sacrificing your time and your very self for the benefit of others (you get benefits too, of course). If done correctly, you will leave people better off than before you entered their lives. The blessing may be in the form of more laughter, a break from a bad day, or a valuable friendship. You go out among the population and create "peak moments" in people's days and they will love you for it and want to be around you. Voila! Popularity.

These may not be sacred moments in the religious sense of the word, but I think the image still fits. You've made someone's day, maybe even life, better and more worth living. That's sacredness in my book (at least this one).

But, as you know, being popular isn't all about sacrifice. Most people, when you give of yourself to them, will happily give back. For example, popular bands give great music and their fans give back in the form of buying their albums and attending their concerts. You may not reach Hollywood level of popularity, but the people you touch on a daily basis will happily give back to you in whatever way they can.

Right now I'm sitting in Tim Hortons finishing up this book. Every time I come in, I make it a point to be friendly and funny with the employees. When they're having a bad day, I listen to them and make them laugh.

Last time I was there, a friend went in and told them I was coming. They put on a fresh pot of coffee for me. When I arrived, they wouldn't even take my money. They just told me to sit down and they brought the coffee to my table, made the way I like it.

This is a perfect example of making sacred through sacrifice and getting a blessing in return. I could've been like the 99.9% of people who come in, order, then sit down or leave. I even could've been like the jerks who treat employees like dirt. Instead, I consistently gave of my time and my personality.

Sure, there were times when I just wanted to sit down and be left alone, but I gave the employees my attention even when they were complaining about being sick or telling me about their boring new apartment search. As a result of my blessing them, they turned around and blessed me in any way they could.

I act like a popular guy everywhere I go, making friends and bringing people into my social circle, so I bless others everywhere I go. And, they, in turn, bless me. Why would anyone not want to be popular when this is what it's really all about?

Now that you've (almost) finished this book, you're on your own (well, mostly). I hope you've come away with the skills to go out and be popular, confident, and ultimately make your world and that of other people a better place. And, if you truly focus on blessing others, you will be popular. And you will be blessed in return. This I guarantee.

Your assignment for this last true chapter is simple. I want you to look back on your newly acquired skills from this book and list ways in which you plan on using them to bless other people as you become more popular.

CONCLUSION

WRAPPING IT UP

I hope you found this book entertaining and helpful. Above all, I hope you found it genuinely life-changing. I want to reiterate that being popular involves a lot of effort (but fun effort), constant practice, and the willingness to adapt under some socially difficult situations. Just reading this book won't make you instantly popular. Going out and practicing what you've learned, mastering it, and above all, making it a habit, will.

And, I hope you actually become popular. I'm not just saying this because you've bought my book and are, in a sense, my student. Believe it or not, I sincerely think that the world needs more outgoing, charming and confident young people who are ready to change the world and positively impact others. I've seen how happy people become when my friends and I interact with them. I've witnessed how lives are changed by simply giving people attention. I've also noticed how the world is a better place when everyone gives, gets, and then gives back in a cycle of blessing others.

Not only that, but I can also tell you from personal experience that being popular is incredibly fun. You meet some awesome people, get attention whenever you want it, and never have to be bored. For example, I know that if I'm having a boring day, I can go anywhere I want and light up the room. Not only that, but as much as I've given, I've gotten more back than I can even express in the form of gifts, opportunities, and above all, friendships. The friendships I've formed in the last few years are my favorite part of being popular.

Your concluding assignment is to list the positive changes you've made throughout the course of this book. I'm sure, if you've worked hard, there are many. Now is the time to write them down and pat yourself on the back. Reward yourself in some way if you want because those positive changes are a real accomplishment. Next, list the areas that still need improvement. Finally, remember that continuing to adapt and grow is crucial. So, I want you to end with the steps you are taking towards maintaining your current level of popularity and becoming even more popular.

If you still haven't quite mastered the material in this book or just want a helping hand in setting and achieving your goals, my colleagues and I will gladly help you out. At *The Popular Teen*, we offer fun events, talks, classes, and consulting to help you become excellent in every aspect of your life. We strive to provide you with the best tools possible for you to become successful and unstoppable. We have websites and books for an older audience as well.

Please visit our website, thepopularteen.com. Also, follow us on social media, including @thepopularteen on Twitter, and on Facebook at facebook.com/ThePopularTeen, so you can receive regular updates with helpful tips and ideas for becoming your best self. If you know an adult who could benefit from our services, or if you want to learn even more, visit thepopularman.com, our brand dedicated to helping guys become more successful.

YOU KNOW YOU WANT TO ASK

1. Who are you anyway? Are you even famous?

I'm Jonathan Bennett, writing along with my brother David, duh. I don't claim to be world-famous, just popular and well-known in my geographical area and other environments. Remember, the odds of being world-famous are tiny. I'm helping you achieve popularity wherever you are right now (likely, high school), which is exactly what I've done in my own life. I've also helped numerous teens and adults find excellence through my teaching, classes, consulting, talks, events, and conferences. Everything in this book comes from my years of research into the science of attraction as well as personal and client experience.

2. *I'm ugly. I can't be popular. Right?*

See Chapter 16. But, to reiterate, you don't have to be great-looking to be popular. You just have to be fun, exciting, and high-value. And give people something they need.

3. *I wasn't popular in middle school or elementary. Isn't it too late?*

A lot of people genuinely become more popular as time goes on. Maybe they develop a new talent or simply grow up. I knew many people in high school who became incredibly popular after shedding some baby fat and kissing the awkward preteen years goodbye. Oh, and look at celebrity yearbook photos sometime. Some people become more popular and famous after high school, college, or even well into their thirties or forties (or later). When I was in 10th grade, I decided to reinvent myself. I stopped being in clubs and social groups that I didn't think fit me, and I started playing football and focusing on being more relaxed and fun. With just a few simple changes, most people didn't even care that a few years earlier I was less athletic and more uptight.

4. *Does this book really work? Is it really this easy?*

Yes and maybe. The book does work. Not only did I follow the techniques outlined here to become popular (both in school and in the present day), but these same principles have helped many of our clients as well. However, the question of easiness is different. If you can follow the principles in this book, then it's actually pretty easy to get people to like you. However, if you've learned bad patterns and habits, then following the principles each day may be challenging. But, the techniques in the book work. Keep trying and don't give up.

5. *Do these techniques work on everyone? The girl in history class just rolled her eyes at me and turned up her nose.*

They do on the vast majority of people. Human nature is pretty straightforward and predictable and these tips will be effective with most people. However, they're not going to work for absolutely every person you encounter. The personalities and tastes of people out there are simply too diverse.

Of course, you'll find people who won't like you, or for whatever reason don't want to interact with you. But for every person you meet like this, you'll find ten for whom these techniques are effective. Besides, your new popular self doesn't worry about people like that girl in history class anyway. And, because you are detached and aren't trying hard to make her like you, she'll probably come around to liking you eventually anyway.

6. *Aren't I manipulating people by using these techniques?*

All language is manipulation. If a realtor says the kitchen is cozy, is it small? It's probably both, but there's nothing wrong with putting the best spin on something. You will be meeting the needs of people and giving them what they want. Just because you know what they need and have methods to deliver the goods doesn't make you a manipulator. Using techniques to connect with others and bless them isn't manipulation, even if you are receiving a benefit in return.

7. What if I don't want to play sports or join clubs?

These tips will work anywhere you happen to be. However, if you are never around people, then the best tips in the world aren't going to help you. You'll have to get out in the world to be effective at meeting people. If you don't want to get involved in teams and clubs, then you'll be at a disadvantage for two reasons.

First, you'll have very little to be proud of and show others that you're high-value. Sitting at home doing nothing (or what others perceive as nothing) won't win you friends. Second, in the high school popularity scene, the easiest way to meet lots of people is to join groups of some kind. Sure, you can meet people the hard way (random encounters away from your natural environments), but joining like-minded groups makes it easier and increases your likelihood of success.

It may be hard to get the courage to join a group or make the commitment to get involved in something. However, it's essential (if you want to be popular), to get out and do it. If you really don't want to join a team or club or nurture a talent, I suspect you're actually operating from fear or laziness and the other reasons are just an excuse. You'll have to overcome this.

8. I'm a gamer and pretty likeable. Why do you pick on gamers?

I have nothing against video games and will sometimes play *Call of Duty: Black Ops - Zombies* when I hang with my buddies, or decompress with some *Angry Birds*.

However, my personal experience with games has been mostly negative. For me, they were escapes that allowed me to avoid contact with other human beings in the real world. I spent one summer when I was nineteen playing video games more than I did going out. I really regret this and don't want you to have the same regret.

Perhaps you keep gaming (and texting, surfing the net, etc.) in perspective, but if you play all the time, I think you may have to seriously evaluate why you're staring at a screen and living in a fantasy land all day. However, I can say this: if you're really, really into games 24/7, there's no way you're living up to your potential in the real world. Sorry, but it's true.

BULLYING IS BULL

This section is for teens or parents who have purchased this book to help with issues related to bullying. While the entire content of this book should help a teen gain the confidence to deter bullying, this chapter specifically addresses behaviors that can empower anyone to stand up to bullying. It also addresses ways that newly confident and popular teens can avoid becoming bullies, and stand up for their peers.

As a teacher, I had to sit through many different discussions and seminars on bullying. One seminar was particularly fascinating (and frustrating). For around forty-five minutes, the presenter talked about ending bullying as we know it.

Then, one of my colleagues finally had enough. He raised his hand and asked how her program of "ending" school bullying was going to undo millions of years of evolution which wired us to be competitive and, yes, even a little bit mean. She couldn't really give him an answer.

To borrow from the words of Jesus, "bullies will always be with us." It's true. Short of isolation in prison or wiping out the human race, you will absolutely encounter bullies.

It's as certain as death and taxes (ask your parents about the tax part). If you're bullied, you have my sympathies. But, I hate to break it to you; bullying occurs outside of high school too.

Anywhere you will go, college, work, church, social events, etc. you will find bullies. You will never rid the world of bullies because it would require you to rid the human race of bad attitudes, prejudice, insecurity, arrogance, and other unattractive behaviors.

For clarity, I've divided this chapter into three sections, one for "victims" (more about why this is in quotes later), another for bullies or potential bullies who think confidence is a license to be a jerk, and a third for confident teens.

For "Victims"

The previous paragraphs may not be the most pleasant thing to read, but don't get depressed. While you can't change other people who are bullies, you can change yourself. You can stop being a "victim," an identity that your teachers and other adults may have even encouraged inadvertently.

Many anti-bullying programs focus on creating "perpetrators" and "victims" and then find ways to keep those two separated. This approach alone won't stop bullying. It will only stop it (and even then, not likely) at school. The only skill the "victims" learn is to ask others for help. That help, I can assure you, doesn't usually come when you go to college or get a job, and encounter even worse bullies.

Also, studies show that school anti-bullying programs not only don't work very well, but may even lead to *more bullying* (15)! It may be that programs give bullies new ideas about how to bully, and train "victims" to be even more reliant on outside help, help which isn't available all the time.

Also, raising awareness about bullying may make people feel good, but does little to affect the social dynamics within a school. So, the purpose of this chapter (and book) is to create empowered teenagers who can confidently be their excellent selves, and as a part of that, stand up to bullies on their own behalf, and on behalf of others. No "victims" here. It's the last time I'm using that word.

Let me begin by repeating some standard advice about bullying that I believe is important.

First, if you are being bullied, don't suffer in silence. Tell an adult, whether it's a parent, friend, teacher or law-enforcement officer. If they don't help you, then tell another.

Second, if you are not finding relief from bullying, then keep talking to the adults in your life, especially at school. It is their job and legal duty to keep you harassment-free. Finally, get help in some capacity if you're feeling depressed, anxious, or suicidal because of bullying (or any reason really). Visit your doctor or talk to a school counselor or other mental health professional. Being bullied sucks and you don't have to put up with it.

When you were a child, you received a series of vaccines that inoculated you against certain diseases like measles. As long as you stayed current on your vaccines, you would be immune to those particular germs.

As a teen (or whatever the age), you can also inoculate yourself against bullying. While these techniques don't mean you'll never be bullied, they will make you less likely to be a target (I'm not using the "v" word) and more likely to be mentally prepared to handle the stress of the bullying.

My first tip is to follow the other tips in this book. There's a reason why this chapter is an appendix to the book. It's not a separate chapter because all the chapters, when applied, help vaccinate you against bullies and jerks.

Bullies typically look for weaker individuals to pick on. They're like wolves taking the easy path by looking for the weak, limping sheep. My understanding of bullying is that it is weak people picking on people they perceive to be even weaker, to help them feel better about themselves. If you are confident, strong, and popular, bullies will be less likely to engage you. They'll likely look for an easier target.

Let me begin my second tip with a story. When I was in high

school, regretfully, I used to bully a friend. My buddies and I would tease him. He would always react very strongly. So, we kept it going because we liked his over-the-top reaction. When he matured and laughed it off, we stopped bothering him.

So, for certain types of bullying (usually shorter-term), sometimes ignoring it or laughing it off can go a long way. If you don't react, many of the non-violent, lazier bullies will simply find someone else who will give them the reaction they want. I know it's hard to ignore someone, especially if that person is being mean, but give it a try nonetheless.

The third tip is not for everyone in this book, but can be very effective. If ignoring doesn't work, you can stand up to the bully. You can do this in any way that doesn't violate laws or school policy. If you confront a bully, make sure you have the personality (and, possibly the physical build and self-defense skills) to pull it off.

Don't appear weak and don't make threats you can't back up either. Always be detached and calm, because don't forget that bullies often love to provoke people to overreact. Stand up in a respectful, but firm way.

If the bully mocks you, respond with something like, "C'mon, Jimmy, you know that's not true, and honestly I need you to stop treating me this way right now." Don't sound stressed, whiny, or needy. Say it confidently and with conviction. Let the bully know you are cool (see Chapter 18), but mean business.

Finally, humor is a great way to immunize yourself against bullying. I was rarely bullied in high school. In fact, I can't even remember an incident. I think it's because I had people laughing and could even get the bullies to like me (or at least tolerate me). The fact that I'd brush off their bullying attempts with humor (some of which they were too dumb to get) and move on to another topic, didn't make bugging me worth their while.

Once again, these tips won't solve a bullying problem, but they should go a long way in helping you become less susceptible to bullying. In addition, following the techniques in this book, ignoring the bully, standing up to him or her, and being funny are also great ways to mentally relax yourself. That means that even if you are bullied, you will be less likely to get too stressed out about it. Remember, you are cool, detached, and excellent all the time, even in the face of pressure and setbacks.

Also, we recommend learning some basic martial arts or self-defense skills (used appropriately per legal and school policy) if bullying becomes too severe. Unfortunately, in the game of life, sometimes standing up to a bully means standing up physically as a last resort.

I have never gotten in a fight in my life, outside of a martial arts studio or gym. But, I am able to verbally stand up to jerks and bullies knowing I have the skills to fight them if necessary. If you are a teen reading this, talk to your parents about getting enrolled in a martial arts program.

Physical altercations are not fun, and unfortunately, in some schools even defending yourself can get you suspended, so it is very important you learn these skills with the guidance of a parent and in line with school policy and the law.

For (Potential) Bullies

I've seen it way too many times with people who ascend the ladder of popularity: they forget where they came from. They spent so much time being picked on by those at the top of the pecking order that when they make it there (or somewhere close), all they know is how to treat others like they were treated themselves.

Instead of becoming confident and attractive individuals, these newly-minted popular kids become cocky jerks or upstart mean girls. Don't do it.

If you want to avoid falling into this trap, I suggest you re-read the final chapter about blessing others (Chapter 38) and remember what popular and confident teens need to do about bullying (mentioned at the end of this chapter). It is always helpful to recall the primary goals of popularity: friendship, attraction, and the joy of being loved by others.

When you were unpopular, those were probably all you really wanted. Don't get caught up in the darker side of popularity, like drama, abuse of power, and manipulation.

I will add that in the long run, such a path will create many headaches. When I was a teacher, many teens who were popular as freshmen were not as seniors. They were fun and cool in the ninth grade, but by the twelfth, they had overplayed their hand by creating drama, bullying, and taking advantage of others. Several didn't finish out their time at the school, since they were thrown out for bullying (it was a private school, so students could be permanently expelled). For some, the police even became involved.

Bullying is taken very seriously both in school and outside of it. So, even if you don't understand the need to bless others, I think you do want to avoid the juvenile detention center. Being Mr. or Miss Popularity there isn't quite as rewarding.

For Confident Teens

If you are already confident and popular, then it is your job to make sure bullies don't harass weaker people. Popularity is about winning over *everyone*. If you are popular, use your confidence and popularity skills to stand up for people that are getting picked on.

This is especially true of popular guys. If you are at the top of the social order at school, you wield a lot of influence over others, both males and females. People look to you as a leader. Remember, *bullies are often weak people picking on even weaker people.* As a confident and strong person, you can easily put bullies in their place.

I have found even saying a simple, "Come on man, that isn't cool" to a bully is enough to do the job. And after that, I'll go up and talk to the target of the bullying to see if everything is "okay" and let him know it won't happen again while I'm around. This is what leaders do.

A good friend of mine was recently at the gym working out. An imposing meathead there was making fun of someone with Down's Syndrome. My friend, not exactly the biggest guy on the planet, stood up to this jerk, telling him his behavior was wrong and he'd better lay off. Not surprisingly, the bully immediately backed down and apologized.

If the popular leaders in every school took my friend's approach to bullies, bullying would end tomorrow.

So, whether you are bullied or turning into a bully yourself, there are solutions. Follow the advice in this chapter and become a cool, confident, fun person who works to make bullying a thing of the past (in your life and the lives of others).

Appendix B

Self-Harm Isn't The Answer

Experts estimate that two million Americans self-harm each year. This is commonly expressed as "cutting" or other forms of bodily mutilation. It may include punching or burning oneself, and even other extreme options (16). The majority of those who self-harm are females under the age of 18, although males do it as well. Some people even self-harm after adolescence.

People give various reasons why they self-harm. Experts believe self-harm may be a way of expressing emotional pain that can't be expressed verbally, or perhaps it's a way of dulling emotional pain with physical pain (the brain processes both in a similar fashion). It may be a way for people to have some control in their lives when other aspects of their lives (such as family life) are out-of-control (16). Self-harm could also be a cry for help or attention.

Parents, teachers, and friends should be on the lookout for signs of self-harm, like scars, scabs, or burn marks. Be aware of attempts to cover the harm, such as wearing long-sleeve clothing all the time (even in the summer), bracelets (especially look for multiple bracelets which cover a sizable area of the arm), and thick make-up on arms and legs.

If you suspect someone is harming herself (or less likely, but possible, himself), talk to a teacher, counselor, or parent immediately. Remember, that self-harm indicates your friend, relative, etc., is experiencing a lot of pain, and getting her help will help her feel better. Letting her continue to cut is *not* what a good friend does.

If you are a parent, and suspect your child is harming herself, be understanding and avoid punishing her. Self-harm is a sign of emotional problems, and should be seen as a cry for help, not as something that needs punished. Make sure you contact a counselor as soon as possible.

If you are harming yourself, know that other coping mechanisms exist that are much healthier than self-harm. Self-harm may temporarily dull some of the pain, but it is not a long-term way to make you happy or end the stress and pain in your life.

Let a teacher, relative, or other trusted adult know about your self-harm (or ask a friend to talk to them for you). A trusted adult can help you find other ways to deal with the pain that don't involve harm to your body. You don't have to continue to suffer. There are real solutions to your problems. Get help in finding them.

Eating disorders can also be viewed as a type of self-harm, and they are prevalent among teens, especially young women. However, men can have eating disorders too. Anorexia, starving oneself by severely restricting calories is common, as is bulimia, binging (overeating) followed by purging (throwing up).

Eating disorders are very serious and can sometimes be fatal. Signs of anorexia include severe calorie restriction, a radically thin appearance, extreme fear of gaining weight, and menstrual irregularities (or complete loss of menstruation). Signs of bulimia include an unhealthy focus on body image, going to the bathroom after or during meals, gorging at meals, and damaged teeth and gums (17).

If you notice any of these symptoms in a friend or relative, seek help immediately. A school guidance counselor or family physician will be able to direct you to appropriate treatment.

If you suspect you have an eating disorder, talk to a trusted adult immediately. As I mentioned, eating disorders can make you very sick and even kill you. That is not something you want to play around with.

For more information on self-harm and eating disorders check out the following websites:

Self-Injury Outreach and Support: sioutreach.org

To Write Love On Her Arms: twloha.com

National Eating Disorders Association: nationaleatingdisorders.org

SOURCES

REFERENCES

Chapter 3

1. http://today.msnbc.msn.com/id/36032653/ns/today-today_health/t/meet-girl-half-brain/#.UENczY1lRig

Chapter 8

2. http://www.denverpost.com/broncos/ci_18784663

Chapter 12

3. http://encyclopedia.adoption.com/entry/pregnancy-after-adoption/285/1.html

Chapter 13

4. http://www.mayoclinic.com/health/stress-relief/SR00034

5. http://www.psychologytoday.com/blog/the-possibility-paradigm/201106/are-you-meeting-your-laugh-quota-why-you-should-laugh-5-year-ol

6. https://www.msu.edu/~jdowell/monro.html

7. http://myweb.brooklyn.liu.edu/jlyttle/Humor/Theory.htm

Chapter 20

8. http://www.ew.com/ew/article/0,,313745,00.html

Chapter 21

9. http://www.celebritynetworth.com/richest-athletes/nfl/brian-bosworth-net-worth/

Chapter 30

10. Cialdini, Robert. Influence: Science And Practice. Boston: Pearson, 2009.

Chapter 32

11. http://www.csun.edu/science/health/docs/tv&health.html

Chapter 33

12. http://well.blogs.nytimes.com/2011/03/23/whats-your-biggest-regret/

13. http://www.dailymail.co.uk/news/article-2106983/We-spend-45mins-week-dwelling-regrets--Electric-Zebra-survey.html

Chapter 34

14. Pease, Allan, and Barbara Pease. <u>The Definitive Book of Body Language</u>. New York: Bantam, 2006.

Appendix A

15. http://ideas.time.com/2013/10/10/anti-bullying-programs-could-be-a-waste-of-time/

Appendix B

16. http://www.mentalhealthamerica.net/self-injury

17. http://www.mayoclinic.com/health/eating-disorders/DS00294/DSECTION=symptoms

TO LEARN A LOT MORE

Below are the resources that I've used and referenced throughout this book, either directly or indirectly. They have also greatly influenced me and the concepts in this book. They have provided concrete tips to increase my overall popularity and success. I highly recommend that you read a couple of these, especially if it's a topic you want to learn more about.

While this reading is not really homework, consider it "extra credit" because you're going above and beyond this book to become an even greater master of popularity. I've arranged them by category. Some of these books are more advanced and are intended for older readers who really want to dig deeper.

Body Language

Driver, Janine, and Mariska Van. Aalst. You Say More than You
Think. New York: Crown, 2010.

Navarro, Joe, and Marvin Karlins. What Every Body Is Saying.
New York: Collins Living, 2008.

Pease, Allan, and Barbara Pease. The Definitive Book of Body
Language. New York: Bantam, 2006.

Changing Your Perspective and Brain-Wiring

Bandler, Richard, and Garner Thomson. The Secrets to Being Happy.
IM Press Inc., 2011.

Bennett, David, Jonathan Bennett, and Joshua Wagner. Say It Like You
Mean It. Columbus, OH: Theta Storm Press, 2011.

Schwartz, Jeffrey, and Rebecca Gladding. You Are Not Your Brain.
New York: Avery, 2011.

Communication and Persuasion

Cialdini, Robert. Influence: Science And Practice. Boston: Pearson, 2009.

Garner, Alan. Conversationally Speaking. Los Angeles: Lowell
House, 1997.

Rosenberg, Marshall. Nonviolent Communication: A Language Of Life.
Encinitas, CA: Puddledancer Press, 2008.

Confidence

McKenna, Paul, and Michael Neill. <u>I Can Make You Confident: The Power To Go For Anything You Want!</u>. New York: Sterling, 2010.

Evolutionary Psychology and Attraction

Badcock, C. R. <u>Evolutionary Psychology: A Critical Introduction</u>. Cambridge, UK: Polity, 2000.

Brizendine, Louann. <u>The Female Brain</u>. New York: Broadway, 2006.

Brizendine, Louann. <u>The Male Brain</u>. New York: Broadway, 2010.

Health, Fitness, and Good Looks

King, Ian, and Lou Schuler. <u>The Book of Muscle</u>. Emmaus, PA: Rodale, 2003.

Roizen, Michael F., and Mehmet Oz. <u>You, On A Diet: The Owner's Manual For Waist Management</u>. New York: Free, 2009.

Roizen, Michael F, and Mehmet Oz. <u>You: The Owner's Manual</u>. New York: Free, 2008.

Mindfulness And Meditation

Kabat-Zinn, Jon. <u>Mindfulness For Beginners: Reclaiming The Present Moment – And Your Life</u>. Louisville, CO: Sounds True, 2011.

Kabat-Zinn, Jon. <u>Wherever You Go, There You Are</u>. New York: Hyperion, 2005.

Popularity

Bennett, Jonathan and David Bennett. <u>Be Popular Now: How Any Man Can Become Confident, Attractive and Successful (And Have Fun Doing It)</u>. Lancaster, OH: Theta Hill Press, 2013.

Success Principles

Bandler, Richard. <u>Get The Life You Want: The Secrets To Quick and Lasting Change With Neuro-Linguistic Programming</u>. Deerfield Beach, FL: Health Communications, 2008.

DeMarco, M.J. <u>The Millionaire Fastlane: Crack The Code to Wealth and Live Rich For A Lifetime!</u>. Phoenix, AZ: Viperion, 2011.

Lieberman, David J. <u>Get Anyone to Do Anything and Never Feel Powerless Again</u>. New York: St. Martin's, 2000.

For more information,
including events, classes, and consulting:

thepopularteen.com

More Excellent Books

By Theta Hill Press:

thetahillpress.com

Be Popular Now: How Any Man Can Become Confident, Attractive and Successful (And Have Fun Doing It)

Eleven Dating Mistakes Guys Make (And How To Correct Them)

Eleven Dating Mistakes Women Make (And How To Correct Them)

Coming Soon:

Size Doesn't Matter: A Short Man's Handbook Of Dating And Relationship Success

Made in the USA
San Bernardino, CA
28 July 2017